W9-ACM-913

Praise for *Rental Person Who Does Nothing*

"Distinctively Japanese musings on meaning and connection."

–Observer

"A beguiling kind of picaresque."

–Times

"Lays bare the bathos and banality of contemporary life... Morimoto, though still elusive, emerges as a modern Bartleby, an inadvertent dissident, someone who has come to see his practice as being 'about enjoying the absurdity of swimming against the tide of efficiency.'"

–Guardian

"Shoji Morimoto's unique memoir tracks the author's life as he refuses work and rents himself out as a passive companion."

–The Skinny

"Undeniable poignancy... A narrative that transcends cultural borders... An eccentric, charming book, showing how humans can connect in the strangest of circumstances."

–Kirkus Reviews, starred review

SHOJI MORIMOTO

rental
person
who does
nothing

a memoir

Translated by Don Knotting

HANOVER
SQUARE
PRESS

HANOVER
SQUARE
PRESS™

Recycling programs
for this product may
not exist in your area.

ISBN-13: 978-1-335-01753-6

Rental Person Who Does Nothing

First published in 2023 by Picador. Originally published in Japan as "RENTAL NANMO SHINAI HITO" TO IU SERVICE WO HAJIMEMASU by KAWADE SHOBO SHINSHA Ltd. Publishers.

English language translation © Don Knotting 2023.

This edition published in 2024.

Hanover Square Press
22 Adelaide St. West, 41st Floor
Toronto, Ontario M5H 4E3, Canada
HanoverSqPress.com
BookClubbish.com

Printed in U.S.A.

rental
person
who does
nothing

Contents

foreword

@morimotoshoji
I'm starting a service called Do-nothing Rental. It's available for any situation in which all you want is a person to be there. Maybe there's a restaurant you want to go to, but you feel awkward going on your own. Maybe a game you want to play, but you're one person short. Or perhaps you'd like someone to keep a space in the park for your cherry blossom viewing party... I only charge transport (from Kokubunji Station) and cost of food/drink (if applicable). I can't do anything except give very simple responses.

With this tweet, I became "Rental Person," a Rental Person Who Does Nothing. At the time, I had 300 followers. Ten months later, I had 100,000. The number of requests has grown too, and now I get a steady flow of about three a day.

I find it utterly amazing. Why on earth has it happened? When I started the service, I thought it might be interesting, but I never imagined it would result in a book, a manga or TV programs. And when I try to hide my surprise, people started talking about my "aura," as though I'm some kind of star.

Readers must find it bizarre. Nobody could have predicted this reaction. After all, I do nothing. I am the type that people get cross with—at home, at work, at a barbecue. Why should a person like that be in demand?

This book is an attempt to answer that question.

If it was written simply by me, I think it would be too subjective. I'm very confused about what's happened and on my own, I'd find it tough to come up with a convincing book. So we tried an experiment. A writer (S) and an editor (T) asked me questions and I gave them very simple responses, and through that process we tried to find an answer. S is not a particular fan of Rental Person. He has written objectively, and in a way that people who don't know anything about my activities can get a clear picture.

So with that as my excuse, I have, as usual, done nothing. I have simply watched, with interest and surprise, as this book has developed.

1. doing nothing

I want to taste a Starbucks hojicha Frappuccino. I like sweet things normally and I've heard that it isn't that sweet, but I'd still like to try it. I don't think I'd be able to drink it all, so would you share it with me? I wouldn't like to leave any.

🐦 @morimotoshoji
I liked this request. It was simple, sincere and a bit sentimental. The client suggested we meet on a weekday, a sunny one, because rain would be a nuisance. That was nice, but I also liked the fact that, in the end, it poured.

Why did I start this Do-nothing Rental service? One reason was the idea of "payment for being" which I saw in a blog written by health counselor Jinnosuke Kokoroya.

My wife follows this blog and I happened to notice that particular expression on her screen. I'd never really thought much of Kokoroya. His solutions always seemed too easy. But some of his sayings struck a chord with me, and "payment for being" was one of those.

Essentially, pay is given for work. It's exchanged for something being done. But Kokoroya argued that people should be paid for just being there—that people have a value even if they do nothing. The idea didn't hit me that forcibly at first, but it sounded interesting. It slipped into a corner of my brain and took root. I began to wonder if "payment for being" might be a real possibility.

Not long afterward, I heard about Pro-Ogorareya, the professional guest, a man whose "job" is having meals with people. He has no fixed address. He just asks people on Twitter to give him food and somewhere to stay. Of the offers he gets, he chooses the ones that look most appealing.

People criticize his way of life. They get angry that he doesn't get a job and feed himself, or they laugh at him, saying he's just a "gigolo." But I thought it sounded like a great way to live. Here was someone being paid for just "being"—proof that it was possible. In that moment, something that had been hidden inside me sprang to life—a wish to live without doing anything. I thought about what Pro-Ogorareya had done—or rather I practically copied his ideas—and before long, my do-nothing service was up and running.

Things can be different simply because someone is there. They don't have to be there, but if they are, something changes. In this chapter, I want to think about some of the requests I've had just "to be there": going to a restaurant with someone who doesn't feel comfortable going on their own; watching a drama rehearsal; sitting with someone while they work; watching someone doing household chores. How do such situations change when a person is rented out simply "to be there"?

I'd like you to think of me sometime tomorrow or the next day. Just say to yourself, "Is she OK?" or something like that. Think of it as support for a newly employed graduate who's had their day

off canceled. There's no very strong reason for this request. I was feeling tired and it just kind of came into my head.

🐦 @morimotoshoji
A request from someone who wanted me to think of them for a moment over the next couple of days. I read the request again and again, because I wasn't sure I understood it. But I accepted it on the assumption that it really was just a matter of thinking of her. I let her know later that I'd done so and in her reply she said that it had had an effect—a response that provided both relief and a degree of worry.

Before I became a Rental Person Who Does Nothing, I did, of course, do something. I'll talk more about it later, but for now I'll give a brief CV. I studied science to post-graduate level and then joined a company that published educational materials and provided distance-learning services. I left after a few years and started calling myself a "freelance writer." I'd been freelance for two years when I came across Kokoraya's "payment for being" idea. By that stage, I wasn't actually doing much writing. I had no respectable reason for this—it was a question of the work being boring and the pay unattractive.

The expression "freelance writer" covers quite a wide spectrum, including advertising copywriters, anonymous magazine and website writers, columnists who write under their own name, and so on. What they have in common is that they make their living through fee-based writing.

My main freelance work was similar to what I had been doing at the company—writing questions for practice test books and explanations for reference books. Besides that, I wrote copy for business pamphlets and summaries of interviews. At first, I just got on and did the work without thinking much about it, but I gradually began to realize how dull it was. I couldn't dissuade myself from feeling that I was doing something that I simply didn't want to do. The job of writing had become stressful.

Of course, the amount of money people are paid for work (in my case, writing fees) depends on the market and no account is taken of the stress involved. This didn't feel right to me. It seemed unfair that people who wanted to do the work, and didn't feel at all stressed by it, got paid the same as people who didn't want to do it and did feel stressed by it. It seemed wrong that I was getting nothing for the mental burden the work was giving me. I can imagine people muttering to themselves,

"Well, there's no such thing as an easy job," and I fully appreciate that there's nothing unusual about work stress. But even so, the situation really bothered me.

Some people may wonder, *Why not look for another job?* That's exactly what I'd been thinking when I left the company. I'd decided to go freelance and only take on jobs I wanted—writing about things that interested me and interviewing people I wanted to interview. But it ended up feeling repetitive. You accept one assignment and you end up doing a series on the same subject, or you are asked to do something very similar for another company in the same field. People are always looking for a good result to be repeated. I found it depressing. I didn't enjoy writing like that. It was stressful to have to meet expectations.

For example, when a company wants exam practice questions, they're looking for a certain standard with delivery by a certain date. If I managed to meet those expectations, then I was likely to get similar work with the equivalent or higher levels of expectation—they might say, "Make the explanations briefer this time," or "How about adding some hints for the students?"

Having these external pressures was bad enough. But there was something inside too. I like to feel my work is fresh and meaningful, so, rather than just re-hashing old questions, I always tried to think of new material.

Unfortunately, though, I'm not that creative and I soon ran out of ideas, which meant I had to do research. I got no pay for this research, but I felt I had to do it, nonetheless. This stressed me out even more—stress that I wasn't paid for. Inevitably there are times when you end up with more stress than pay. That's when I don't want to do the work. And that's the reason I've given up all the jobs I've ever had.

Hey, Rental Person! I'd like to go and sit in the park in the evening breeze with a can of chu-hai but I think I'd look a bit odd drinking on my own. Would you mind coming along?

🐦 @morimotoshoji
I accepted this request last night and was given a lot to drink. Summer, nighttime, a park, alcohol— it was a powerful mix. I got pretty drunk and I haven't quite recovered. I'm supposed to meet some people today, including a YouTuber I retweeted. I'm sorry if things don't go to plan.

Without abandoning my freelancer work, I started a blog. I thought that with a blog I'd be able to write what

I wanted, and maybe I'd stick at it. But I grew short of material and didn't really want to spend my life hunting up stuff to write on a blog.

I told myself to be a grown-up and stick to something, but the stress always got too much. I'd try to alleviate it somehow, but that never really worked. I was in a repetitive cycle of trying to do something and ending up doing nothing. Eventually, I began to realize that doing nothing was what suited me best.

By this stage, I was hardly writing at all, so how did I make ends meet? The answer is, I was doing some financial trading. It looked like an easier way of making money than writing, and I did have a bit of success. I suppose at the time I was looking for ways to live without doing anything.

I don't do any trading now and, looking back on it, I realize that it was pure luck that I made any money that way. If I'd continued, I'm sure I would have lost a lot of money somewhere down the line. Or maybe I'd just have got fed up and chucked it in.

I don't ever get fed up with my do-nothing role, and there's no stress. Why? I could come up with several answers to that, but the simplest one is that there's variety; the people and the situations are different every time.

It's like watching TV. A lot of people find TV boring,

but I like it (though we don't have one). You can just sit around doing nothing while the TV churns out entertainment, news and commercials. I find it gives me just about the right degree of stimulus. Do-nothing Rental gives me a similar kind of passive entertainment, even though in this case I'm the service provider, rather than the service user.

I've dropped a bit of washing (and its hanger) from my flat to the flat below. When I first moved to this building, I got a lot of complaints via the property manager about children running about, and the neighbor often came up to complain in person. I addressed the situation each time and I haven't had a complaint for about six months. Even so, I'm nervous about going to get the washing and wondered if you would come with me.

Request: to come and stand behind me while I ask for my washing back. Then listen to me talk about it afterward in my apartment.

 @morimotoshoji
The client has had frequent trouble with the tenant downstairs and didn't feel safe meeting

them alone. They had no one else to ask on the day, so they contacted me. The washing was retrieved, but the situation remains awkward and the client still feels scared.

Both my writing work and my blog had become dull and routine. There was no easy fix. I found it very difficult, even impossible, to find the variety, the new stimuli, that I wanted. But now stimuli and variety are provided by others. It's very easy.

I leaped blindly into this do-nothing service. I didn't know what would happen, but I had a feeling it might lead to interesting things, and that's the way it's turned out.

Did I have any resistance to spending long periods of time with people I didn't know? The simple answer is "no."

When I was a freelance writer, I used to attend what we called a "philosophy café." About ten people who didn't know each other got together for two hours to discuss serious questions like "What is freedom?" "What is love?" and "Can violence be justified in the name of justice?" I enjoyed it. I used to hate talking to people at school or in the company—people who were part of the same fixed community. But when I went along to the philosophy café, I found myself talking readily with people I didn't know. I felt comfortable in a community that existed just for the moment, with simple, temporary relationships uncomplicated by past or future.

I split up with my boyfriend last year. I really liked him and I'm not completely over him. On the 13th it will be exactly a year since he was unfaithful to me— that was why we split up. I don't have the confidence to spend the day on my own, but I think it would be too much to drag out a friend on a Monday night. I wondered if you would mind going for a drink, or something.

 @morimotoshoji
We went to a nice Italian place in Shibuya. If this was a late-night TV drama, you might have expected some kind of romantic development. As it was, we had a bit of pizza and went our separate ways.

People tend to think that personal matters should be spoken about with those who are close friends, lovers or

family members. But since starting this do-nothing service, I've learned that there are a lot of important things
that can be talked about with people you don't know
very well or even at all.

Depth of discussion and depth of relationship don't
always go hand in hand. The fact that you're very close
to someone doesn't mean you can necessarily open up
to them. In truth, closeness quite often makes people
keep their mouths shut.

I get a surprising number of requests to listen to people.
I've been told secrets of a very personal and serious
nature. They left me wondering, *Why me—a complete
and utter stranger?*

The way I see it, talking to someone about one's troubles means showing that person one's weaknesses. So if I
consulted someone I knew well—someone with whom
a relationship has developed through time and who will
probably be part of my life in the future—that person
would always know my weaknesses. If the relationship
remains positive, then that may be OK. But relationships
can deteriorate, and if this one does, then the person's
knowledge of my weaknesses could put me at a disad-
vantage. They could reveal them to others without me
having the slightest idea. This could cause real problems.

As Rental Person, I have only the flimsiest connection

with my clients. I am practically transparent. Unless they make another request, we'll probably never meet again. They have a story they have to tell and it's my role to be there while they tell it. In one of Aesop's fables, a character longs to tell a secret and so tells it to the reeds. I'm just there, like those reeds. I may describe the situation on Twitter, but I never give details that would allow the clients to be identified, so there's very little chance of any weakness they reveal to me becoming known to others.

Another reason why people ask me to listen to them seems to be that I don't give advice. One of my clients told me they hated it when people responded with unsolicited advice. They didn't like to feel that what they said was being evaluated. Even positive responses like, "Great!" or "That's interesting!" could put pressure on them.

I think I share that kind of feeling. If I tell someone something, I don't like it when they say things like, "Oh, that's OK. It's nothing to worry about." How can they judge whether it's OK or not? They don't have complete information. I've only told them part of what I'm feeling. I've only put part of it into words. It's not possible to give a completely accurate picture of what one is feeling inside. *Don't judge me!* I want to say. *You don't know anything about me.*

Of course, I know they're well-intentioned and that I'm being very unfair. But that doesn't stop me thinking the way I do—it just makes me feel guilty about it. And because people have good intentions, it would be very awkward if I gave any indication of what was going through my mind.

This all makes me want to avoid ever talking to people about my problems. So when I listen to clients, I try not to evaluate at all. I just nod and say something along the lines of "Uh-huh" or "I see." Fortunately, not many people who want to be listened to ask me for advice. Occasionally, though, people do ask to consult me about relationships, for example. When that happens, I explain in advance that I can't offer any advice—"advising" would be "doing something." But if they are satisfied with me just listening to them talk, then that's OK.

I'll talk more about "listening" requests later on.

I think this do-nothing service can often have a catalyst effect. A catalyst is a substance which speeds up a chemical process, without undergoing any change itself. Manganese dioxide is often given as an example. If you add manganese dioxide to hydrogen peroxide you will produce a lot of oxygen. The hydrogen peroxide will gradually give off oxygen anyway, but adding manganese dioxide speeds the process up.

Having someone with you can have a similar effect. You (hydrogen peroxide) may take ten units of energy to do something on your own, but with someone else there (manganese dioxide) you may be able to achieve the same result with just four or five units of energy.

Going into a restaurant, doing your job or housework and so on—these are things that can be done on your own, but people may have difficulty getting going. Do-nothing Rental can be a catalyst that helps people get on with things.

Another "accompanying" type of request, similar to going to a restaurant, is going to an event. If it's something like an all-standing concert, I may not be with the client the whole time. We go in together, but after that we may act independently. But even then I think the arrangement to go with Rental Person has acted as a catalyst, reducing the amount of energy the client uses to achieve their goal.

Here's an example that highlights the catalyst effect:

Happy New Year! I'm doing Good Morning Tokyo on January 4 and I wondered if you might be free

to come along. It's the same place as last time—
Inokashira Park, 8:30 to 9:00. I'm planning
something special to celebrate the start of the year!

🐦 @morimotoshoji
Today I've been to Inokashira Park to watch a
woman dressed as a boar greet people as they
walked past.

The client often does this kind of thing, spending a while
in the park before going to work, dancing about and saying, "Good morning!" to passersby. She makes her own
costumes and when I saw her before, she was dressed as
something else. Her message the first time said, "Basically, I do this on my own, but I thought it might be fun
if you were there in front of me!" Then she added, "I
figured you must be odd like me, so I thought it would
be interesting to meet."

Anyway, I went and watched her again, and when
she'd finished she said, "I'm not embarrassed to dress
as a boar, but I do feel a bit lonely performing like that
and I have to keep myself going. It's easier to do it if
there's someone with me." Mind you, there was a TV
crew there at the time, and this comment was actually
directed at the camera.

★ ★ ★

With these "accompanying" and "watching" requests, my role is really, of course, just to be there. I say "watching" but that doesn't mean my eyes are always on the client. I may be looking at something else entirely. The clients accept this.

I'm an amateur writer and at the moment I'm writing a novel. When I'm writing on my own, I often get a bit lazy, so I'd like someone to watch me. I wonder if you would sit in front of me while I work. I may say something to you occasionally, but basically I'd just like you to sit there and pass the time.

🐦 @morimotoshoji

The client was finishing off a manuscript for submission to a new writers' competition and wanted something to keep him going. On his own he was lazy and spent too much time on Twitter. I just sat there reading some manga books that he provided. He said he made better progress than usual and that it had helped to have me (someone he didn't know) in the room, especially having explained to me his rules of working.

This request said the client might talk to me occasionally, and in fact this happens quite frequently when I am "watching" people work.

A manga artist client said, "If I have an assistant with me they worry if I break for too long. They say things like, 'Shouldn't we be getting back to work?' It's nice to be able just to talk in a relaxed way like this."

Of course, "talk" in the context of this do-nothing service is not a two-way process. All I can do is give basic responses, and I know nothing about clients' work. A manga artist is drawing pictures and a novelist is writing stories, but I don't know any details of their work. All I can see across the desk is the back of their computer.

It's very similar when I "watch" a rehearsal. The request is just for me "to be there." I don't go along to learn, observe or comment. That's why I've never hesitated to include reports on rehearsal-watching on Twitter. Of course, there are times when it's awkward to do absolutely nothing. When I was watching one rehearsal, I was asked to participate for a while, as there was a scene in which an actor had to talk to a member of the audience. In those particular circumstances, I felt it was OK to be involved, as I could simply give the actor my normal basic responses. This rehearsal was by a group of five or six who'd rented a room in a small community center. Just as with the writer and manga artist, having someone there they didn't know seemed to add a bit of positive tension.

I like the kind of request where I'm really asked just "to be there." It means I can do something else at the same time—responding to Twitter messages, say, or surfing the net.

Sometimes the client gets what they want without me even accepting their request.

Something bad happened at the beginning of this year and since then I've been unable to do anything. I've been mentally and physically exhausted. I couldn't go out and couldn't do any housework. Recently, I've been trying to get back to my old self, cleaning and making a schedule, and so on. There are a lot of "items" in the flat—dishes, pots and pans. [...] I want to wash them. I'll be shouting and screaming as I do it, but I really want to get them done. I'd like you to be beside me (or rather, hiding outside on the balcony). I simply can't do it when I'm on my own. If I could just get these items put away, I feel I'd be one step closer to being an ordinary human being.

@morimotoshoji
A request to be with someone shouting and screaming while they did several months of dishwashing. I couldn't really face it, so I refused, but I just got a message from the client to say they'd got the dishes done on their own. Maybe mentioning it to someone had helped them to see the situation objectively and to act calmly. An unusual case in which the required effect was achieved without the requested visit.

This was a typical "watching" request. However, the client was going to ask me to be outside on the balcony because the flat was "unhygienic" and there "might be bugs." I'm not a cleanliness fanatic, but I decided I'd better refuse, as I do have a problem with unhygienic environments and I don't like bugs. But a few days later, the client sent me a message saying, "Everything's cleared up and there weren't any bugs. Thank you very much!"

My feeling is that by telling me they'd decided to tidy up the kitchen, they'd triggered a change in attitude, which enabled them to get it done. I knew the reason they didn't tidy up wasn't because they were too busy, but because of an obstacle within them. A problem of some kind had put their head in a spin, and they couldn't settle down to anything. I guess writing a DM helped them control their thoughts, gave some order to the chaos, and perhaps made it easier to take action. Anyway, in this case, Do-nothing Rental seems to have functioned as a kind of catalyst simply through messages on Twitter—an extreme example of doing nothing.

Here's another case where there was a positive outcome in spite of my refusing Twitter requests:

On December 23, 2019, I got the same request from three different people. It was the Emperor's birthday and, as every year, he was going to wave to the public in the imperial palace grounds. Each of the requests was to accompany the client to this event. I wasn't free that day, so I turned them all down, but I was rather excited to get multiple requests for the same thing, so I reported it on Twitter, to which someone responded, "Why don't they all go together?" The three of them saw this suggestion, and in the end that's what they did. So their hopes of going with someone to the palace were fulfilled after all, without my even being there. It certainly wasn't an outcome I'd expected, and it was interesting to see the kind of ripple effect Do-nothing Rental can have through Twitter.

One client said this do-nothing service was like a wild card you could play once in your life, or if you didn't play it, it acted as a good luck charm. Well, I don't mind how often I am played, and I think I'd say that, rather than a lucky charm, I'm more like an escape route. But if people feel Rental Person's existence gives them any kind of strength, I'm really delighted.

> 🐦 @morimotoshoji
> Now and then I get requests to do things like taking photos, helping tidy up or buying something. I stubbornly fend them off. Don't forget there are other ways of renting people. If you want someone to do something for you, try Ossan Rental.

According to its website, Ossan Rental "rents out middle-aged men who mistakenly think they're cool. Prices from 1,000 yen an hour. They're at your service for chats, confidences and running errands."

I'm sometimes asked by clients and followers where I see the line between doing "nothing" and doing "something." It's very difficult to explain. I don't have some kind of internal rule book. All I can say is that I decide case by case.

Though I can't give a comprehensive definition of what I *will* do, I can give examples of what I *won't* do. I refuse any case where it looks as though I'll have to use my own judgment. This includes lining up to buy something or running an errand, even where I have been given directions or orders. On the other hand, I would probably accept a request to keep a place for a cherry blossom viewing party, assuming that I'd go with the client and they'd choose the place in the park they wanted to reserve. Then I would be nothing more than a person sitting on tarpaulin sheeting until the party started.

Sometimes, I have an awkward situation where I accept a request that sounds OK, only to find I've made a mistake. The main reason is that I get fed up with it. I once accepted a request to line up with someone outside a pachinko parlor. I did it once, and that's enough. I don't want to do it again.

In a lot of jobs, being able to repeat the same kind of activity is a selling point. As I mentioned earlier, this was the case when I was a freelance writer: "I've written this kind of article in the past (so please give me more of the same)." But with this do-nothing service, I quite often reject requests on the basis that I've done it before.

For example, I received consecutive requests to go to Aikatsu Friends card game tournaments, where players must participate in groups of two. I told the second client that I'd had exactly the same request before and that if I got a different, interesting-sounding request for the same time, I'd prefer to accept that one. I hoped that would be OK. The client said that would be fine. In the end I didn't get another request, so I went with the client to the tournament.

I've turned down a number of requests to go to pop concerts too. I don't know much about music, and most of the concerts I've been asked to go along to have been by artists I've never heard of. At first, I thought it might be fun but it wasn't really—if you're not interested, you're not interested. The range of artists was impressive, but once I was used to that, I got a bit bored and lost my enthusiasm for going at all. I might feel differently if the concert is by a famous artist that even I've heard of, like Morning Musume or Paul McCartney. So, again, it's case by case.

I'd like you to come for tea at a café or restaurant, talk a bit and watch me while I do some tasks online.

I've got to think seriously about getting married, but I can't get started. I suppose I'm used to my life as it is and don't want to face reality. I have a lot of friends who are single and I find it difficult to let on that I'm looking for a husband. (I'm the type to say I can live without a man!) I know I can't go on like this, but when I'm on my own I just follow my geeky hobbies, or if it's a day off I celebrate by staying in bed. So nothing gets done. Could you watch me as I do some computer work—get info together, register on marriage partner sites, send out messages, apply for parties, etc.? AHHHHHHH! I'll be in agony while I'm doing it, so it would be great if you could talk just a little.

 @morimotoshoji
A woman wanted me to watch her as she started her unenthusiastic husband-hunting activities. She applied herself steadily to the task of registering with agencies, etc. She screamed (like in her DM) every ten minutes or so. At one stage, she made a mistake with an app, clicking "Like" for a man she wanted to skip past. She stared up at the ceiling and looked very upset. I had a great afternoon tea and really enjoyed myself.

When I used to go to the philosophy café, I had fun listening to people I didn't know, and I feel similarly when I'm dealing with "accompanying" requests. As Rental Person, of course, I only give basic responses, but clients generally talk about this and that and I enjoy hearing what they have to say. In fact, this is another reason

I don't prioritize concerts—while the music is playing, clients can't say much.

I want to make it clear that I don't feel any stress at an event I'm not interested in. If I'm at a concert, I'm always near the client or next to them if seats are reserved, but that doesn't mean I have to be looking at the stage if I don't want to. At the moment, though, I'm getting more and more requests to go to concerts and generally I refuse them. Rather than fill my schedule with concerts, I prefer to keep time free for other requests. If concert requests stopped coming completely and then one suddenly came up again, I might accept it; the idea might seem fresh again. So the line between what I accept and what I turn down is a vague one.

Some people may be doubtful that writing a book can be classified as "doing nothing," but, as I said in the foreword, the actual work is being done by someone else. All I have provided are "simple responses" to questions. When I say "simple," I mean they're based on what I already know. I haven't done any special preparation for the book; it's just a series of those simple responses. From that point of view, I think that, for me, it really is "doing nothing."

🐦 @morimotoshoji
When I left an appointment halfway through because I wasn't interested, the client blocked me.

I've only once ended an appointment early because I wasn't enjoying it. The client asked me to attend an event they'd organized. It involved a number of people going up in turn onto a podium and talking about a dream they wanted to turn into reality. The audience assessed their content and presentation skills. The person who got the best assessment would receive support to make their dream come true. There was nothing suspicious about the event at all—everything seemed entirely proper and genuine. But the moment the organizer started his introductory speech, I felt uncomfortable. "I am sure there's nobody in the room who doesn't have a dream," he said. "Every one of us thinks about the future." *Not sure I do*, I thought. His words felt pushy and repressive.

After about half an hour, I began to think, *If I stay here any longer I'll end up writing something negative on Twitter*. So I sent the client a message, saying I was sorry, I wasn't in the mood and was going to leave early. I'd pay my own travel expenses. I received an acknowledgment, but then my account was immediately blocked.

I feel very sorry about what happened. It was stressful for me to leave halfway through, but I felt the burden of staying would have been even greater.

Why did I think this talk of "dreams" pushy? Looking back, I think it was a kind of prejudice. My impression is that people who talk about dreams in such a public way take a very moralizing stance: that a "dream" should be for the benefit of others—for the benefit of the world.

At the event, one of the speakers said they wanted to support disadvantaged children in Africa. Of course, it's best if children living in harsh conditions are helped, but I don't think I'd want to talk to someone like that— someone who could stand up and tell an audience about their philanthropic dreams. I wouldn't know how to react. I'd feel the pressure of all that goodwill.

That doesn't mean I have a negative feeling about all dreams. If I was asked what my dream is, I'd respond immediately: "Living without doing anything." That's what I want, and it's not for the benefit of anybody else. I think that's enough for a dream. Perhaps it's unkind of me, but when I listen to people sounding off about their grand dreams, I tend to be suspicious that they're looking for praise.

★ ★ ★

Normally when people talk about a "dream" in this sense, they're referring to something to be achieved in the future. So being asked about dreams can be depressing for people, forcing them to think about the future. My dream of doing nothing is already a reality, so in fact, it is a dream of keeping things as they are. Why shouldn't a dream focus on the here and now? Why is there an assumption that it must be about the future?

Though I don't like looking ahead, I once had a request from a university student who wanted me to listen to his worries about the future. As usual, most of the time I only responded in the most basic ways, but when he asked me, "Is there anything you'd advise me to do while I'm still a student?" I said, "No, I don't think you have to do anything." This reply seemed to be what Rental Person should say; it was also what I really felt.

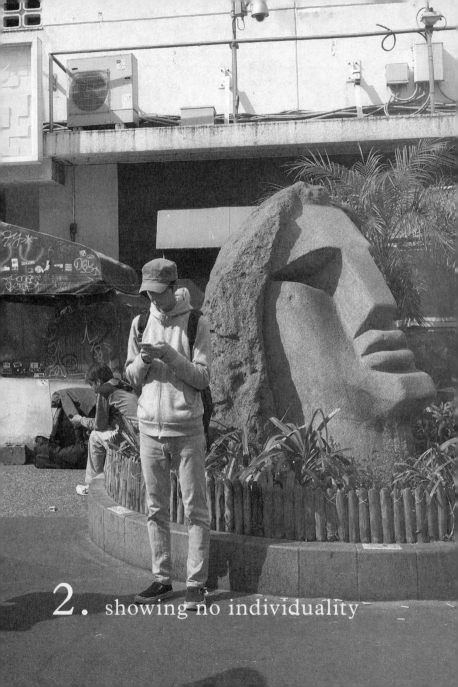

2. showing no individuality

It's my second year at this company, which I joined when I graduated from university. I don't get on with my boss and sometimes we argue. The atmosphere is tense and I feel a bit scared about going to work tomorrow morning. If possible, I'd like someone to travel with me. Would that be possible?

 @morimotoshoji
A request to accompany someone on their morning commute. The client has a bad relationship with her boss and is scared to go to work. She developed a stomachache after a "terrible meeting." Having dropped out of a job

myself after three years, I felt very sympathetic
and got up early to join her. Companies can be
terrible places.

"It makes no difference whether you're here or not."

"I can't tell whether you're alive or dead."

"You're a permanent vacancy."

These are the kind of things my boss used to say to
me. It was his way of mocking me, I suppose. It irritated
him that I didn't have a strong personality, that I had no
influence on those around me. I guess he wanted me to
be a positive force in the company, a dynamo who made
things go well, a strong leader.

But as I said earlier, I'm very bad at communicat-
ing with people in a fixed community, like a company.
When going out for drinks after work, I'd often sit in
silence, not speaking to anyone, and then I'd be teased
about it. Perhaps I was supposed to make my presence
felt by building a warm atmosphere—refilling people's
drinks, or doing something to bring the boss and his
younger colleagues together.

I think people who can't make this kind of contribution often have a handicap in life. But for Rental Person,
it's a plus and I think that in its own very different way,
Do-nothing Rental provides something positive to quite
a lot of people. Take the "accompanying" request at the

start of the chapter: the client wants to do something and I just go along. No deep commitment is expected and no personality required. It's the complete opposite of what was expected of me at my previous company. It's funny that someone like Rental Person should be in demand. I suppose you could say my lack of individuality has become my "product."

But paradoxically you could also say that this do-nothing service has given me more individuality.

So what is individuality?

Simply speaking, I suppose individuality can be divided into two sets of qualities: those that you have naturally—your face, body, voice and so on—and those that you acquire—special talents, communication skills. Individuality is generally thought to be a positive thing, but it's a very vague and abstract idea. It exists in a context of comparison; it's a relative value that emerges only when a person is part of a group.

Nobody wants me to be "individual" when I'm Rental Person. Take the example of my very first request:

Hello! I saw your tweet so I thought I'd send you a DM.

Would you meet me in about an hour at Kokubunji Station? I'd like you to come for a walk and have your picture taken. It would take two or three hours, or until you've had enough. I'd like you to carry a balloon. Apart from that you'd just be walking, talking, standing still, etc. You wouldn't have to do anything else.

 @morimotoshoji
My first client asked me to hold a balloon and have my photo taken. They also asked me to do some Instagram promotion. It was fun walking with the balloon from Kokubunji to West Kokubunji. I kept the balloon and was quite unpopular on the commuter train back. I enjoyed that.

If I had been a very individual person, this request might not have worked. I might not have managed to do what the client wanted. It was a school graduation project, and the star of the piece was the balloon, so I had to be someone who wouldn't take attention away from the balloon. Being so ordinary, it was easy for me to take the role of "person with the balloon."

Somebody once asked me to join them in a purikura photo, which allows you to play around with your appearance. I hadn't much experience with purikura and wasn't familiar with its latest developments, so when the screen said "MAKE A HEART-SHAPE TOGETHER," I frantically tried to hold up my hand in the shape of half a heart. The client stopped me. "We won't bother with that," she said. She was more interested in having me as a bit of background. Again, anonymity was what the client was after. Anyway, it was good fun.

> **@morimotoshoji**
> The other day I went to meet a client at the agreed location. She'd told me she'd be wearing a long, bright skirt so when I saw someone dressed like that, I went up and said hello. But it was someone else and they walked straight off. When I have a client appointment, I always introduce myself by saying, "Hello, I'm Rental Person." I guess it would be quite unsettling to have a stranger come up and say that if you're not expecting it.

I always wear very ordinary clothes that don't make any statement—a plain T-shirt or sweatshirt with jeans or chinos. If there's anything to mark me out, it's that I always wear a cotton cap. After I'd been wearing it for a while, I realized that it makes me look like a workman.

I never used to have a cap. I began wearing one in May 2018, about a month before I started this do-nothing service. I suddenly thought I'd like to try one sometime, so why not now? I wandered into a headgear shop in Kichijoji and the shop assistant suggested the type of cap I now wear.

I put the cap on and set off home. It felt good. I'd never liked Kichijoji much, because the streets get so crowded; that day, though, I felt more comfortable than usual. I think one reason was that I wasn't bothered by people looking at me. I could see the brim of the cap above my eyes, and I felt as if that was blocking out people's gaze. I know that in a crowd like that nobody was really going to look at me, but self-consciousness is difficult to control. Another advantage of the cap was that with a restricted field of vision I could be more introspective, hiding away in my own world.

I think this easy introspection, and the sense of freedom from people's gaze, helped me to be honest with myself, to face up to the feeling that I wanted to do nothing. Saying that, I may be overplaying the role of the cap, but it was certainly very soon after buying it that I hit on the Rental Person idea, so perhaps the two things are related. I'm sure that feeling free from people's gaze helped me to move on. And looking back now, the fact that the shop I happened to go into was called 無 (*mu*, "nothing") feels a bit like fate.

My cap has been surprisingly useful since I started this

do-nothing service. Aside from the obvious practical functions of warmth, protection from wind and rain, and hiding unruly hair, it also serves as something for people to look out for when they are meeting me, and best of all, it makes me look like a workman or deliveryman.

Cap-wearing delivery staff are a very common sight in Japan, and though, of course, I'm not wearing a complete uniform, I think my cap helps clients relax. I feel it gives a reassuring formality to our relationship, which is nice for me too. Although they don't know me at all, it's as if there's a kind of manual allowing them to handle the situation with minimal communication. And when the job's over, I just go home, like any workman. So I think I was very lucky that the first bit of headwear I bought wasn't a hat, a beanie, or a baseball cap—just a work cap.

And for me, the cap is useful if I want to block out a client's gaze, or to shut down completely. So, although it may not be very polite, I don't take the cap off even when I introduce myself to clients. Or perhaps I'm so reliant on it that I'm embarrassed to take it off at all.

Sometimes clients are pleased for me to show individuality when I'm not directly engaged with their request.

For example, someone asked me to go with them to a baseball game and, with some time to kill, we went to a café. While we were there, the client asked if I'd talk about math. I believe that talking about things I know falls within the definition of "simple responses," so I started off by talking about cardioids and how they explained the curves visible on the cups of tea in front of us. I carried on talking about math and physics for quite a while and the client seemed to enjoy it, saying "Don't worry about the game. Just keep on talking." When I'd run out of things to say, we went to the stadium. The game was already half over, but we still went in and watched the rest, so from that point of view, I did manage to complete the assignment.

I wouldn't feel comfortable, though, if people contacted me under the impression, or misapprehension, that I could do X or Y, or knew a lot about Z. If they had that kind of expectation, they'd evaluate me on that basis after meeting me. They'd start saying things like, "He didn't know that much" or "He wasn't particularly interesting." If people see me as a specific character with a certain set of qualities, then they'll be disappointed when I don't turn out to be what they expect. So what I really want as Rental Person is to have no defining attributes—no good points, no bad points.

*Hello! I'm a first-time requester. I'm sorry it's very
short notice, but could you manage a request today?
I'd like you to come and have an ice-cream soda
with me in a café. I'm thinking of somewhere near
Shibuya Station.*

The client was male. Although his request was sudden,
his desire for an ice-cream soda was longer-term. I knew
how awkward it can be for a Japanese man to go into a
café on his own and order an ice-cream soda, so I said
"yes" straightaway. We sipped our sodas with pride.

As a result of this episode, I developed a reputation for
liking ice-cream soda. It became part of my personality:
"Rental Person likes ice-cream soda." I played up to it
for a while, I suppose, writing ice-cream soda tweets.
When people bought me an ice-cream soda, I began to
feel that I was drinking it for them, behaving in the way
they expected me to. After a while I got fed up with it,
and so I tried to dilute my ice-cream soda image, tweeting that I'd decided to switch my allegiance to lemon
squash. I think it's good to tweet about changes like that.
It makes Rental Person seem human.

While not having much individuality fits with "doing
nothing," there's a danger that a complete lack of indi-

viduality could end up as a strong identity in itself. So it's good to have a bit of noise or interference on the line. And anyway, I'd find it stressful to try to be someone with no individuality at all. So when I tweet about changes or when I use a bit of blunt language, I'm not only trying to stop a fixed character forming, I'm also relieving some stress. And looking at it from a strategic angle, I send tweets about the switch from ice-cream soda to lemon squash, or changes to my cap and jacket, and so on, as symbols of changes to the Do-nothing Rental service itself as it evolves.

I am contacting you to ask if you would be prepared to observe court proceedings. The case will be heard in January at the Tokyo District Court (Chiyoda-ku). It relates to a civil action and the defendant is Tokyo University. I look forward to hearing from you.

 @morimotoshoji

A request to observe court proceedings. The message is from the plaintiff and Tokyo University is the defendant. The plaintiff claims to have been the victim of "academic harassment." On the completion of a master's degree, a professor asked them not to continue their studies. They are suing on the basis that they were obstructed in their plans to study for a doctorate. Having to face the professor in the courtroom, they feel it would be a help to have someone in the visitors' seats who knows the situation.

As Rental Person, I don't have to display individuality and I don't try to. But when I was looking for a job, even I had to turn a spotlight on my own personality. Filling in forms and having interviews meant trying to sell myself. I had to know what my strong points were and express them in words.

I didn't have many friends as a postgraduate, so to fill in application forms I just referred to a "how-to" manual. I didn't put in much effort; even so, writing about my "strengths" made me feel ill. Think about it for a moment. If someone starts telling you how wonderful they are, it turns you right off. But when you're trying to get a job, that's what you have to do. There's no choice. You identify your "good points," call them "strengths" or "personality." Then, according to recruitment advertisements and websites, you're supposed to build a career around them, "working in your own way," "doing what only you can do." But is life really like that?

I don't remember much about what I wrote in the application forms; I think I squeezed out something about "giving form to ideas," based on what I'd done in my research at university. It was pure fabrication really, wrapped up in nice-sounding words. I was already going out with the girl who is now my wife, so I did some interview practice with her as the interviewer, but I didn't enjoy it. I loathed absolutely everything about job hunting. Looking back now, I see that it made me lie a lot. Perhaps that makes me sound like a victim.

I think that when I was looking for a job, I felt exactly as I do today—that I don't want my identity to be defined by a set of abilities.

In a sense, this is at the heart of this do-nothing service— I'd like the world to be one where even if people can't do anything for others, even if they can make no contribution to society, they can still live stress-free lives. This is very important to me because of the gap that exists between the value that I sense in people and the value assigned to them by society.

I'll talk a bit about myself.

I have an older brother and an older sister. Or "had" in the case of one of them. My brother, the eldest, messed up his university entrance exams and became depressed. He's over forty now and has never had a job. My sister had a very tough time trying to find the right type of work. She didn't get the job she wanted. It hit her very badly and she killed herself.

Maybe their exam and job-hunting failures were not the root causes of their unhappiness. Perhaps they were just triggers that speeded something up or precipitated a decline. When life doesn't go according to plan, stress can take many different forms, particularly at their stage of life.

I was at school at the time. I felt the value of my precious siblings being warped and eroded because of the expectations of society. From society's point of view, were they "productive" in any measurable way? The answer must be "no." I suppose my siblings and I grew up in a relatively carefree environment and never had any major problems to face when we were small. Maybe because of that, we didn't worry too much about developing the skills that society demands, so when we were exposed to society, we had to try that much harder.

My sister's specs as an adult weren't what the companies she applied to wanted. For me, though, she had value simply because she was there. Gaps like that in their perceived value can be a huge source of stress for anybody who, by society's standards, doesn't seem able to do anything. People can die because of the stress of adapting to society. Or they can lose every ounce of their energy. I've seen it happen.

If people are pressured by society into saying they have particular abilities, then the true value they have as themselves becomes blurred. If you say you have value because you can do particular things, you will always be judged by established social standards. So I never say I can do anything. And I don't do anything.

Today I left my tenth job. I feel very negative, like I'll never be able to work again. I thought it might help to mark this occasion and go for a hamburger at the place I first worked. Would you come with me?

@morimotoshoji
A request to eat a hamburger to mark someone leaving their tenth job. The client wants to get over their worries about working in the future. While we were eating our hamburgers, they told me all about the various jobs they'd had. They looked miserable when their eyes were on the staff.

It seems to me I've made my choices in life by a process of elimination. This means I've focused on what I can't do rather than what I can; what doesn't interest me rather than what does; what's painful rather than what's enjoyable. I've narrowed things down by eliminating the negatives. By drawing a line that separates things I can't accept, I form a picture of my "self" and then my real feelings become clear.

For example, when I decided to order lemon squash at a café rather than ice-cream soda, this wasn't so much because I wanted lemon squash but because I was fed up with ice-cream soda. When I am clear about what I don't want to do, a plan falls into place. So by discarding possibilities one by one, avoiding things I can't do or don't want to do, I've ended up with a life "doing nothing." At least, for the moment.

How many people in the world contribute to society through a job they'd predicted would be perfect for their personality? Even if you manage to come up with a dream of what you want to do, you can't expect much to come of it. Negative reactions like "I can't do it" or "I don't want to do it" seem more intuitive, a kind of physical reflex. I think that acting in line with these reflexes is in some ways a more honest approach to life. Or at least maybe all my judgments about whether something is OK or not, whether to accept or reject a proposal, are based on physical reactions. There's always something physical or instinctive about my decisions on Rental Person requests. And this type of reflex or instinct works best when I'm faced with something I don't like. When I tweet about these reactions, when I say, "I don't like this type of thing," I think that's when my individuality shows most clearly.

Here's a well-known line from a manga for boys: "When you talk about yourself, say what you like, not what you don't!!!"

Most people treat these as wise words, but not me. It's a line I really hate. I can't stand people who say things like that. What's wrong with talking about what you don't like? People who speak about themselves in terms of what they like are often very vague and dull. They sound as if they're just trying to make a good impression. People who talk clearly about what they dislike tend to be more interesting, focusing more on specifics. They're probably more honest. Maybe more sincere.

🐦 @morimotoshoji
A request to eat with a client in preparation for a New Year party with colleagues. The client wants to get used to eating with people. I imagined she must be extremely shy, but in fact she suffers from a very specific syndrome. When eating with people she's not used to, she develops symptoms

such as nausea. She's run out of excuses not to go out with colleagues.

I'm on my way home from the New Year party. After you came to eat with me, I managed to tell my boss about my condition. He was very considerate and chose a venue that made things easier for me.

@morimotoshoji

The client with the eating syndrome sent a message to say she'd got through the New Year party without problems. Apparently, having told me about her condition, she'd found it easier to disclose it to people around her and she'd received a lot of consideration. She also told me she'd been encouraged by the messages that others with the same syndrome had sent in response to my tweet. A positive effect of Twitter.

I guess some people might say that by making decisions through elimination I'm limiting my own possibilities in life. But in the past it seemed to me there were too many possibilities. Or I was under the illusion that there were. It was very confusing. In reality, there was almost nothing I could do, but I kept thinking, *maybe I can do this* or *maybe I can do that*, without having any clear idea what I should do or what I'd be suited to. By narrowing the scope of possibilities, I began to understand what I wanted and, in the end, realized that my only choice was "do nothing." Now, as Rental Person, I enjoy life and have no conflict with anyone.

What possibilities did I think about before discarding them?

While at graduate school, I thought I might be a researcher, or work my way up in a company. I thought I might win a prize for a novel I'd write in my spare time, or even become a successful comedian—crazy fantasies like that.

Probably the most realistic of these was becoming a researcher.

I studied physics for my first degree and went straight to graduate school, where I was in the Earth and Planetary Materials Science Group, researching earthquakes. I programmed earthquake simulations, analyzing statistical frequency and cycle trends. But it never seemed to me that research would ever enable people to predict earthquakes. With a pessimistic view like that, I couldn't feel very motivated. And I started believing that if earthquakes couldn't be predicted, then death could come at any time. Although I'm sure everybody has a similar vague anxiety, in my case it was stronger and more specific.

Before long, I had to make a decision about my future. To be a researcher meant staying at university and I knew there were many more gifted people there than me. And I wasn't exactly gushing with enthusiasm anyhow. In fact, there were lots of reasons not to pursue that idea. I felt myself rejecting it in a physical way. A feeling of aversion and disorientation overcame any desire I had to be a researcher. That's the kind of person I am.

Hello

I'm getting divorced. My wife is leaving on Sunday, January 27. I'd like to mark the event by going to have some soba the following day at Fuji Soba in front of Kokubunji Station. Will you go with me?

 @morimotoshoji

A request to join someone for soba the day after his wife moved out. He'd seen my tweets about accompanying a woman to file divorce papers, and taking her example had decided to do something positive to mark a difficult juncture in life. He said he'd chosen Fuji Soba because they weren't pushy. Fuji Soba promotes itself as providing taste and service you can trust. He muttered something about "trust" as we finished the meal.

I'm happy with this do-nothing service. I think I'm suited to it. As I said before, I don't have much personality, and I'm very ordinary to look at—neither handsome nor ugly, not too stylish or shabby. I'm just a neutral, harmless figure in a crowd.

I also find Rental Person interesting. I'm curious about things—not very curious, just curious. A broad kind of curiosity, but not a deep-seated one. I receive quite a lot of requests from people with intense and specific interests. They may be devoted fans of some pop idol, for example. I like to find out why they are such big fans, and when I meet them, I always find myself amazed at their enthusiasm. Personally, I'm not the type who has a special interest in particular things—if I'm asked about my interests or hobbies, I struggle to identify them. I can find almost everything interesting. For example, in the last chapter, I mentioned an Aikatsu Friends tournament—a game event based on an anime I'd never even seen. I got a bit fed up with it in the end, although going along was absolutely fine.

People may be surprised to read something like the following from a customer-facing business owner, but as the proprietor of this do-nothing service, I didn't find it odd at all:

Hello. I recently opened a café. The hours are 11 to 4, but almost nobody comes at 11 so I just can't be bothered to prepare the place for opening time. Would you mind coming at 11 and sitting there quietly drinking something? Thanks!

It's in Shinjuku. The tea and coffee are very good!

I can understand how she feels. It must be a pain opening up when you know there won't be any customers. I'm not good in the mornings myself. When I worked at a company, it always took me a long time to get going after I clocked in. So I liked the sound of this request.

I arrived five minutes before opening time and was a bit worried to find the shutters completely closed. I was relieved to find the request was genuine when the owner came trotting up at 10:58 and we went in. Just after 11:00, though, a number of customers arrived. *That's odd*, I thought as I drank a nice cup of café au lait. *Not much point me being here.*

Hello. I suddenly feel like giving people money. Can I send you an Amazon gift card?

 @morimotoshoji
Hello. OK.

Thank you!

 @morimotoshoji
Thank you!!!!!

 @morimotoshoji
The client suddenly felt like giving people some money so asked me if he could send an Amazon card. I said that would be okay, of course, and then received a 5,000-yen card. I replied with five exclamation marks. A lot of nice things have been happening to me since the start of the year. I don't know why.

I tend to get a lot of likes and tweets when I give glimpses of my real self on Twitter. Normally I write

68

tweets in a detached manner, though sometimes I express feeling and I am maybe a bit blunt, which triggers a response. I get tweets that read: "I didn't realize you were so human. I like you for that." Apparently, one sign of humanity is getting excited about receiving a gift card. Many people described my reaction as "cute." I suppose it's not surprising that Rental Person followers thought I wasn't interested in money, but I think everyone wants money. When I let my feelings slip into tweets from time to time, they tend to become a type of branding. I don't mind this happening, although, as I've said earlier, I consciously try to avoid acquiring a "character."

One very important factor that makes me suited to the Rental Person role is that I have a family. This gives people confidence that I am not going to do anything odd. That's what people tell me. So I put the information out on Twitter whenever I have a suitable opportunity— thirty-five years old, with wife and child.

To be honest, when I started this do-nothing service, there were moments when I was worried, or hopeful, that a woman I was meeting might come on to me. But, fortunately or not, it's never happened. Somebody once suggested sex through a DM, so I replied that I was married and wasn't interested, to which came the response, "Get a job, then, dickhead!" I wasn't too pleased about that.

I thought I might get asked to watch someone masturbate; that hasn't happened either. I have been asked to watch a couple who'd met online having offline sex. It would have met the criterion of not doing anything, so it seemed a possibility, but my wife said it sounded disgusting and asked me not to, so I didn't.

🐦 @morimotoshoji

I met someone recently who, inspired by "Rental Person Who Does Nothing," was operating as "Rental Person Who Does Anything." Apparently, he's already given up, because he only got requests for day labor.

Soon after I started Do-nothing Rental in June 2018, several similarly named accounts appeared on Twitter. One claimed to be good at listening and another promised to be entirely nonjudgmental. It was an interesting experience for me to have imitators. At the same time, I felt uncomfortable—there was something rather false and pushy about the accounts. I told my wife about them and she said she didn't like the sound of anyone

who said of themselves that they were good at listening.
I broadly agree.

And although I described these accounts as imitators, I wouldn't say that their approach to listening is the
same as mine. Lots of people want me to listen to them,
but when I listen, it is always in a passive way. I'm not
doing anything—I'm just hearing what they say while
I'm with them. But the "imitators" were promising active listening services. Of course, once this do-nothing
service was established, an imitator would have to dif-
ferentiate themselves in some way, and to add a service
like that would be to move right away from the basic do-
nothing idea. It becomes a service like any other in the
world, based on "doing something." Services and jobs
have always been like that. The novelty of Do-nothing
Rental was to turn that idea on its head. From this point
of view, they're not really imitators at all.

There was one Twitter account that copied the idea of
"doing nothing" very directly. It may sound conceited,
but I didn't think very much of this imitator. The person
didn't seem to have written anything interesting and I
don't think I'd want to meet him. I had a very different
reaction when I heard about Pro-Ogorareya, the professional guest I mentioned before. I thought he must
have had some very interesting experiences and I really
wanted to meet him. He had a lifestyle that no one had

ever thought of before and I figured it must have taken a remarkable person to make the idea a reality. That is why he's attracted attention. Actually, I regard myself as his imitator.

I work at a church. I wondered if you would come to church one Sunday. Most people at the church just come on Sundays and go to work or school during the week, but in my case, my place of work is my place of worship too, so my circle of acquaintances is small. You always think things are interesting so I thought it would be nice if you came to a service. It would be fun for me. I'd be perfectly happy with just simple responses. I hope you will think about it.

@morimotoshoji
A request to go to a church service. Working and worshipping at the church, the client has a limited circle of acquaintances. When I arrived at the church the client introduced me as "Do-nothing Rental." The man at the door said, "You don't have to rent anything, but shall we lend you a Bible?"

a rental person day

This is how Rental Person spent a day:

'I want you to watch me practising on a horizontal bar.'

Meet at South Entrance, Shibuya Station by the Moai figure.

Usually I'm meeting people I don't know, so it's normally at a station or a landmark.

9:45

The client is a new elementary-school teacher and is having trouble teaching horizontal bar exercises in PE. She doesn't think she's good at them, but can't practise at school as the other teachers will see. So practice was in a children's play area in a park. Whenever children came, she stopped and gave them priority. But she managed to get through her practice. Then we sat for a while on the swings. She seemed more confident.

11:00

Lunch

Not much time till the next request, so a quick snack. Ate a rice ball while answering DMs.

(2)

'I'd like you to listen to me talking about the future.'

12:00

A client from the music world who's reached a crossroads in life. He's moved around a lot and doesn't feel he has stable relationships with others in the industry. Rental Person doesn't meddle in people's futures so I just listen.

'I feel better.'

'I'd like you to come and see the cherry blossom with me and have a bento meal.'

2:00

A repeat client asking me to eat a home-made bento-box lunch. Like last time, I was given some extra food to take with me. I'm looking forward to having that at home.

(3)

(3)

Reply to DMs on the way to the next request.

'I'd like you to come with me to a temple.'

(4)

4:30

The client is moving overseas with her family. As a final memory, she wants me to stand with her as she prays for safety for her household. After watching her I prayed for my household too.

I've got to do the washing when I get home.

6:00

Home

3. not getting too close

I've got a great girlfriend, but I can't really talk about her to my other friends so I wondered if I could talk about her to you. I'd really like it if you could say things like "she sounds nice" from time to time while you're listening.

 @morimotoshoji

A client wants me to listen to them talking about their "great girlfriend"—the request is from a woman. Not many people know she's a lesbian. She'd tried coming out to someone but they ended up saying things that upset her. They didn't mean to, but she found it hard to carry on talking.

She contacted me because she thought I wouldn't say anything that would upset her.

Since I started this do-nothing service, I've been surprised to discover that there are so many things people want to talk about but can't. At least, they can't talk to people they know. They talk to me, though. People I don't know at all, people who, at best, I might have sat opposite on a train or brushed past in a crowd, will talk to me about very personal matters.

As I've said, I receive many listening requests and when I listen, I normally give only minimal responses. Even if the client hasn't specified that they want me to listen to them, I often find myself doing just that. They might ask me to join them for an activity—going to a pop concert, a karaoke place, or maybe a pharmacy—and on the way they'll start telling me about their jobs and interests and what they feel in their daily lives. Perhaps they're worried I won't like silence. They remind me of actors on a stage. In reality, of course, they're just walking or driving a car, but to me they seem to be standing in a spotlight. Even when they're describing tiny details of their lives, it's as though they're telling me a dramatic story. For that moment, they have the magnetism of a real actor on a real stage. Often, I find myself listening so intently that we arrive at our destination without me even realizing.

I've never felt this kind of thing with people I know. With friends, even if you're chatting away without anything better to do, you don't reveal everything, and you don't talk about yourself nonstop. You want to give the other person a chance to speak, so you ask them how things are going and listen to what they say. You have to keep a balance to maintain the relationship.

Just meeting once allows people to get up on stage without embarrassment. To me it seems a new way of relating to people.

It's not just listening requests that put me in a role that would normally fall to a close friend or relative. I've been asked to accompany somebody as they file divorce papers, to say goodbye on a railway platform, to wait at a marathon finishing line, and to pay a hospital visit. People make such requests quite often. What is it that they want from me, a complete stranger?

When people ask me to listen to them, the topic is often something that they feel they can't talk to other people about. Here's a case I remember well, where the subject matter seemed particularly sensitive.

The initial inquiry was: "There's something to do with my upbringing that I feel very sad about. I can't tell anyone else, so if possible, I'd like to tell you." Sometimes when people want me just to listen, we go to a café, but when it's a very private matter, I often go to their homes—this was one such case. It was just before Christmas and the streets were bright and bustling as I walked toward the client's home.

When I arrived, we had some drinks and chatted for a while, and then the client said very apologetically, "I'm sorry. I don't think I can talk about my problem today. I've still not really come to terms with it, you see."

"OK," I said.

I didn't leave straightaway, though, and before I knew it, I'd been there for four hours. I thought I'd better be on my way, but as I stood up to leave, the client said: "There are quite a lot in Russia, apparently," and with that puzzling remark he started to talk about how he had once been a member of the Aum Shinrikyo cult.

He'd joined the sect with his parents when he was a child and remained with it until 1995, when the cult's leader, Shoko Asahara, was arrested for masterminding the sarin nerve gas attack on the Tokyo subway, in which thirteen people died. He had been a member of Aum's successor organization for a while, but by the time I met him, he had completely withdrawn from that too and was, he said, working at an ordinary company.

He wanted to admit he'd been a member of the Aum sect because he had strong feelings to express. He thought the executions on July 6, 2018, of Asahara and six other members of the sect's executive were unjustified. He seemed very angry. Talking about the Tokyo and other incidents, he said, "I don't think Asahara-san actually gave the orders… I wanted to hear the truth from his own mouth… You can't hear the truth from a dead man." According to him, everyone at the sect had been kind. He mentioned specifically Yoshihiro Inoue, another of the Aum leadership, who was executed on the same day as Asahara. "Inoue-san did a lot for me," he said with a mixture of warmth and deep sadness.

I could certainly see why he couldn't tell people about his past. It must have been very tough for him. He'd changed his name to hide his identity, but that didn't solve everything. He said he was jealous of people who could talk about themselves in the conventional way—which university they'd been to, which club activities they'd enjoyed there, what job they have at which company—the kind of information that people spontaneously come out with by way of self-introduction. "I don't know what to say about myself," he told me, "and I feel guilty when I make things up." He didn't have a past that he could tell people about; the past that had molded him into what he was today—his childhood memories, where he'd lived, the people he'd been brought up among—this real past couldn't be mentioned, it had to remain a secret.

I once tweeted as follows:

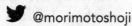 @morimotoshoji
Someone has asked me to listen to something they can't say to other people. They've tried talking to acquaintances and Ossan Rental, but it didn't really work. They found that when there's an existing relationship, or when payment is involved, the listener makes an awkward attempt to sort the problem out and an uncomfortable sense of hierarchy develops.

Followers sent me these responses:

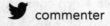 commenter
Intervening often does more harm than good. When a situation is stable, an offer to "sort it out" is really an offer to "stir things up." I think this person will be better off just being listened to by you.

commenter
I've just started with Ossan Rental, and I really feel it's important that the man says he won't try to solve anything.

These responses reflect exactly the way I feel, so I won't add anything.

Here's another client who had something extremely difficult to talk about.

I want to know how I feel when I'm with another living creature. Would you be prepared to spend between six hours and a day with me?

The client had been living alone for so long that he'd forgotten what it was like for there to be someone else in his space, so he wanted me to spend quite a long time with him in his house. Actually, his request message included something more: "There is something about my background I have always had to hide. I'd like you to hear what it is. I can't tell anybody else."

The first part of his request was met, I think—at least, the visit seemed to have had a positive effect. He seemed happy and reassured to find that his sense of taste was not odd. He drank quite a lot and as the alcohol flowed, he also provided some homemade dishes—barbecued pork slices and kimchi, as well as octopus with wild parsley sauce, which he prepared there and then. They all tasted good and he beamed when I told him so. "I'm glad you like them!" he said. He had a small fridge full of drinks and he told me to take whatever I wanted. I met up with him in the morning and must have spent about six and a half hours in his house, with a constant supply of food. Maybe because I was there so long, he eventually remembered to close the door when he went to the bathroom.

We'd been chatting for quite some time when, finally, in a very offhand way, he started talking about his hidden past. "I was in a juvenile offenders' institution when I was a teenager," he said.

"Oh yes?" I said, nodding as I normally do.

"Well, yes," he said quietly. "Actually, I…er…killed someone."

From the moment I'd first seen him, I'd assumed that he was a professional—a doctor, or something like that. He was well organized and looked successful. I was amazed that a person like him could have killed someone. Somehow it really took me aback to think that a person who cooked so well, who gave an overall impression of competence, could have such a dark past.

The incongruity had a real impact on me. In a way, I was very moved.

Since then, I think I've looked at people in a different way, realizing that even the most ordinary, upright-looking people may not be what they seem.

People often ask me if I find it tough to listen to people talking about distressing matters. To be honest, it doesn't affect me at all. In fact, I'm asked the question so often that I feel myself wanting to question the assumptions behind it. Do people normally find it difficult?

People might think I'm cold for saying this, but when I'm listening to clients, I'm thinking, *That would be interesting to tweet*, or *Good, that's great material*. Maybe I'm less emotional than other people, or perhaps I'm simply not affected by other people's emotions. I think this makes me suited to being Rental Person. I don't get too involved in the client's world. If real listening is a matter of getting very close to the other person, tuning in one's feelings, then that's not what I do.

Or maybe the reason I don't get affected by the difficult matters my clients talk about is that I'm not spontaneously very imaginative. I find using my imagination hard work, so I tend not to. And it seems to me that however much you use your imagination, you can't really understand another person.

Somebody suggested that because I don't give clients much of a response, they tend to develop their own idea of what I'm thinking—picturing a reaction that suits them. If they're sad, they can think I want to comfort them; if they're happy, they can think I'm sharing that happiness. In feeling that someone's agreeing with them or understanding them, maybe people grow more confident in themselves, even if the listener is a complete stranger. If I were to talk more, then my reaction would be clearer, leaving the client less scope to imagine how I'm feeling.

I'd never really thought about that kind of thing before. I suppose that's because I'm not naturally responsive. It doesn't really matter to me what people do or say. Perhaps that's why I get such a variety of requests.

Although it may be an odd analogy, some creatures, such as peacocks and jewel beetles, have structural color rather than fixed color. Instead of pigmentation, they have a physical structure that refracts light to give the impression of color, and this color changes according to the quality of the light. Maybe that's what Rental Person is like—someone whose appearance varies according to the viewer's angle or wavelength.

People ask me if I don't feel like giving up and going home when I have a client who is boring or unpleasant to be with. I suppose they think I should be getting something positive from my free time—I'm not being paid, so at least I should be with someone whose company I enjoy. In fact, I never normally think of leaving early. On Twitter I say that I may leave early, but once I'm on my own with a client, it's too much of a hassle to get up and leave. It's not a question of the client's feelings, it's a matter of avoiding stress. I've never had a client who was so unpleasant that I felt I had to get away, whatever stress that would involve. I can't really imagine having a client like that. I think that if a case was going to be really uncomfortable I'd get a sense of that from the request message and refuse to take it up in the first place. The only exception was the event when people spoke about their dreams and it got too much so I had to leave.

Perhaps I can only behave the way I do because of my policy of normally only seeing clients once. The situation would probably be very different if they were people I knew long-term—relatives, colleagues or classmates. Perhaps it's not just me who feels security in seeing someone just once; maybe some of my clients do too. I'm not sure, though, as not everyone lets me know how they feel.

@morimotoshoji
After a recent assignment the client said: "It was great. People often seem to worry that I'm not enjoying myself when in fact I am, so, I just wanted to say I really had fun." I knew exactly what he meant. When I go drinking with a group and I'm having a perfectly nice time, people sometimes say things like "You're not saying much. Are you OK?"

@morimotoshoji
When I'm asked to listen to somebody talking about their problems, they often start off with a phrase such as "It doesn't really matter much, but…" If something's troubling someone and they feel that people aren't going to take it seriously, they feel stuck.

They can't express their problem because they think they'll be laughed at, so they just keep it locked up inside. Some misfortunes are obvious, and we can all see that they'd be tough to handle, but there are many smaller, less conspicuous problems that can also be very tough in their own way.

People who want to tell me things they can't say to other people often start by saying their story's a bit trivial or boring. But it isn't boring at all.

For example, sometimes I'm asked to listen to someone talking about a band or an anime film they like. They say they're not obsessive fans and don't know that much about the subject, yet they still want someone to listen to them. When I hear them, I often wonder what, objectively, could be stopping them talking to other people. Maybe they worry they don't know enough for their opinions to be worth listening to, but still have an urge to say what they think. I can understand that. I like Spitz and, though I don't know all their albums, I sometimes feel I want to talk about how much I like them, but I think I'd hesitate before actually doing so.

With friends, a conversation generally stays within expected parameters. There's an understanding that you talk about certain things. Talking to a friend who shares a particular interest—pop singers or computer games, for example—it's normally best to keep on that subject. If you start to veer away, the friend may lose interest. This is a rule that, consciously or unconsciously, people seem to follow. A new subject you raise may be genuinely boring for your companion, or, if it's private and involved, they may feel uncomfortable, making the situation embarrassing for both of you. Everyone has to accept there are times when they can't talk about what they want to talk about. In those situations, Rental Person may be a solution.

How do people feel after telling me things they can't tell others? Many are very positive, saying things like "It's a relief," or "I'm glad I told you," or "I enjoyed talking to you." This was the kind of response I got from both the client who'd been in the Aum sect and from the client who'd been in the juvenile detention center.

On the other hand, some people say things like "Well, talking about it doesn't really solve the problem." Then, maybe to keep me happy, they sometimes add, "But it was good to be able to talk." Nobody so far has complained that it's been a waste of time and that I've done nothing for them. After all, "doing nothing" is what people expect from me.

So, broadly speaking, there are people who are clearly happy afterward and there are people who still feel anxious. Those who still feel anxious seem to me to be people who wanted some kind of advice. But, as I keep saying, that's not something I can give.

Some people who haven't been clients wonder if putting problems into words may actually aggravate a situation—making clients feel the problems even more deeply. I've never really had that impression, but I suppose the following case wasn't far off.

*I wonder if you could come and meet me off a plane
at Narita Airport on Wednesday, December 19.
My granny died on the morning I left for a period
of study abroad and I couldn't go to the funeral. I
was very fond of her. I'll be visiting her grave after
I get back and I'll be feeling sad when I arrive, so it
would be nice to have someone waving at me when
I get to the airport.*

 @morimotoshoji
I went to the airport as requested. I'd never met
the client so I couldn't react very spontaneously at
the arrivals gate, but she'd made it quite easy for
me to recognize her and as soon as I did, I waved.
I'm not sure whether I was any mental support
to her, but I suppose I did provide practical
support by looking after her luggage while she
was getting other things sorted out.

After she arrived, she said she'd like to sing and to talk
to me about her grandmother, so I went with her to a
karaoke box. She sang for a while and then started talking. Her granny was really kind, she said. There were

two large fridges in her granny's house, both crammed with different types of ice cream and Popsicles. She was allowed to take anything she liked at any time. Then she explained how she hadn't seen her friends for ages and didn't want to talk to them about her sadness at not being able to go to the funeral. That was why she preferred not to have them meet her at the airport. I can understand that. As I've said, I think that talking to someone about a problem is to put your weakness in their hands. Maybe that's what she had in mind.

The client didn't seem at all sad when she arrived, nor when we were on our way to the karaoke box, nor when she was singing, but after she started to talk about her grandmother, she gradually became more emotional and, in the end, she began to cry. Probably, talking about her grandmother's death made her face it, accept it as something she should be sad about.

Of course, there's a big difference between someone reminiscing about their lovely old granny and someone confessing to having been a member of Aum Shinrikyo. But both clients were saying things that were hidden inside, things they didn't feel they could talk about to others. When people do that, sometimes the pain is relieved and sometimes the cut grows deeper. Of course, I can't see inside people and tell which will happen in a particular case. It depends on the individual.

★ ★ ★

Although these were all interesting assignments, to be frank, if I were in that kind of situation myself, I probably wouldn't want to be with anyone, and I have sometimes wondered whether I should really accept requests of this type.

It's not that I don't respect the way the clients feel. In ordinary relations, people will often be with someone because they care about them or because they sympathize. It's tough being with someone if you don't automatically feel sympathetic or you're not sure how to show consideration. It's awkward if you don't understand what it is they want to talk about and don't know what to say. As Rental Person, though, I don't have to comfort anybody and I'm never asked for sympathy. When I've felt that just being there may help a bit, I've accepted the request.

I don't always feel entirely comfortable with these cases, but as long as the client is sincere I think it is my role to accept them.

One important role normally assumed by close relatives is hospital visits.

Hi!
I'm in hospital. Would you come and visit me? I've
been here for a month and none of my family has
come to see me. Feel free to use my real name. Bring
along some lunch for yourself and I'll pay for that as
well as your travel.

This was a request for a hospital visit, but the situation was rather unusual. The client had been hospitalized after a drug overdose and was in a suicide-risk isolation unit. There's not much to do in an isolation unit because they don't allow any cords—you can't watch TV, you can't have headphones, and you can't even have a charger, so access to the net and social media is limited, though nurses will charge your phone for you if you ask them.

When I arrived at the unit, the client came straight up and asked for my signature. There was no suitable paper, so she made me sign the information booklet in the room. We played a board game to pass the time; I won so easily I was worried that she might be depressed. She seemed OK, though, and started talking enthusiastically about her favorite brand—Black Brain Clothing—which features drug-related design motifs. She was wearing a Black Brain T-shirt with a photo of the designer being taken to hospital after an overdose of his own. He'd taken the photo himself—apparently, you can still sometimes take pictures after an overdose.

It was very interesting to see what an isolation unit was like and to hear what had happened to her. In fact, I almost forgot that the purpose of my being there was to visit her as a sick patient. I think it did feel like a proper hospital visit for the client, although I was a complete stranger.

The client had bipolar disorder, and so was subject to repeated mood swings, but, physically, she had no problems at all. For her, being in an isolation ward meant too much spare time, and my being there helped fill some of it up. So I think my visit was positive from that point of view and she certainly looked satisfied. The experience made me realize that a hospital visit doesn't necessarily have to be by someone very close, though I think it depends on the type of illness and the mental state of the patient.

People in hospital seem to have far more time on their hands than I ever imagined, and the isolation ward must have been particularly tough. Previously, I'd always thought of having time to spare as a good thing—this was a kind of hell.

I don't normally do this, but at the end of my visit I asked if I could come again. I felt sure that the client had appreciated my being there and that another visit would not be an imposition.

I had originally planned to come with a TV crew, but the director of the hospital was going to be away on the day I was coming so it was difficult to get permission. If possible, I wanted to come back on a day when the director would be there, so that it would be easier to ask if the visit could be filmed.

But my main reason for asking to come again was that I had enjoyed being there. I found myself fascinated in that strange environment listening to the client's experience. When I asked if I could visit again, she said "Will you? Yes please!" Well, I suppose she was in a manic phase so perhaps she would have welcomed whatever I said.

Here are my tweets from after my second visit.

🐦 @morimotoshoji

I went to the hospital again today. I got a lot of messages after my first visit, and so, it seems, did the client. She said there were messages of support, as well as questions such as, "What's Keio University Hospital like?" and "Any spaces in a multi-bed ward?" She showed me her treatment bill before she'd seen it herself. (It was quite reasonable.)

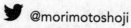 @morimotoshoji

Her doctor put a block on social networking sites and stopped any visits from people she doesn't know (I was excluded from the ban because I'd met her once before). She was in a major manic phase after the social media reaction and didn't sleep all night, and then felt exhausted the next day. During this manic phase, she canceled the lease on the flat she'd been in when she was hospitalized and took out another. Her energy amazed me.

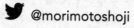 @morimotoshoji

She's made a very important decision, which I can't explain here, but it was interesting listening to her talk about the doctor's reaction. "How can anyone in such a small space cause such a furor?" he'd said. I realized that even in an isolation unit you can go very wild if you have the internet.

I had another visit request from someone of about seventy.

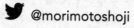 @morimotoshoji

I spent the morning in a care home. I'd been asked by a client to spend some time with his younger

99

brother. The home was for old people, but he was younger than my parents. He'd been paralyzed in an accident of some kind, but there was no problem with conversation. He told me to bring two funny stories and two riddles next time—so if anyone knows any riddles...

Although the man was almost bedridden, his brain was very active and he ate properly. Being paralyzed and mentally healthy, he had a lot of time on his hands. The client had said his brother enjoyed talking and he wanted me to listen to him.

I felt a bit uncomfortable at the idea of going to a care home, but I figured it would be something to tweet about, so I thought, *OK, just this once.* When I got there, though, I did feel stressed because of the way the staff looked at me. Anyway, I met the client outside and went with him straight to his brother's room. Before long the client got up and left. I stayed with his brother for several hours.

His brother had worked for a travel company as a tour guide and had spent much of his time flying around the world. He had a large stock of stories about all the places he'd been and he was short of people to tell them to. I suppose he spoke to his brother a lot, but maybe his brother couldn't spare enough time, or perhaps it felt odd for stories like that to be told by one brother to another.

I enjoyed hearing about his experiences around the world, and as usual I just nodded or said things like "Oh really?" Eventually, there was a period of silence, which he broke by asking if I wanted to hear a riddle. He told me one—I can't remember it now—and I had a go at answering it. I didn't have any riddles to tell him in return, so when I finally got up to leave, he said, "Make sure you bring some riddles next time."

I haven't seen him again and without being asked, I can't really go (I didn't ask to come again when I was there); at least he did say "next time" and I felt he was being genuinely friendly, so I think my visit had a positive effect. When I first arrived, he'd stared at me as if to say, "Who the hell are you?" but when his brother told him to talk to me, he seemed to accept the idea easily enough. I'm not sure he ever quite realized what I was doing there, though. He seemed to assume that I was looking for a job and told me more than once that if I kept trying, he was sure something would turn up eventually.

One client once asked me to walk with him along his old route to primary school. He wanted me to listen to him talking about his schooldays. He'd been bullied and the trauma remained with him, but he felt he couldn't tell

101

anyone. He felt he might overcome the trauma by going back along his old route and speaking to me about what had happened.

While we were walking, the client kept his head down and didn't smile at all. When we reached the school gate, he brightened up and was suddenly talkative. He pointed at the school building and yard and fondly recalled the music room. He seemed absorbed in memories that were unconnected to bullying.

He himself said he was undemonstrative and, looking at him, it was difficult to tell what was going on inside. But I think that by the end of our meeting, his spirits had been lifted.

It struck me that when handling a very heartfelt request like that one, I become more anonymous; the sense of being a social media personality falls away. If someone's talking about their troubles to a complete stranger, then the worse those troubles are, the less it matters who the stranger is. In these cases, it's not a matter of using Rental Person as a bit of fun, it's just a simple desire to have someone there.

Some people tell me that my activities are very much like those of a listening volunteer, and that is true to an extent. Listening volunteers don't criticize or argue with their clients and they don't express strong opinions.

I don't either. But then I don't do anything—I simply stay with a client for as long as necessary. So, although there's an overlap, you couldn't call me a "listener." And I have no real way of knowing whether a client has resolved any trouble or trauma. In this last case, for example, I don't know for sure whether I was any help— you'd have to ask the client if you wanted to know how he really felt.

Here's another case of someone asking me to go with them to a place from their past. There was no mention of a trauma this time.

We moved around a lot when I was a child because of my father's work. We were in Tokyo from when I was five till I was nine, so the place we lived there has a lot of memories for me. The house has been demolished and I don't have the courage to go there on my own. It would be a great support to have someone with me, but I hesitate to involve a friend who doesn't know all about it.

I'm nearly thirty and I want to go back and meet my childhood self. I think it would be a great stimulus for me. I wonder if you would mind coming with me.

🐦 @morimotoshoji

The client wanted me to walk with her around where she used to live as a child. It was fun having a personal guided tour—"There was a nice dentist here... That salon's still going! I had my hair done there for a special visit to a shrine when I was seven... It took so long!... This is where I noticed my mother following me the first time I went out alone with a boy." But when we reached the plot of land where the house had been she went quiet. Nothing remained of it at all.

As we were walking along she said she was glad she hadn't brought a friend. She didn't seem to know how to express her feelings, and I think it would have been difficult for a friend to know how to respond. She didn't have to worry about all that with me, though—I say I do nothing, so she expected nothing.

Here's another request that many people might think would more usually have gone to a family member. In this case it had a catalyst effect.

Are you free on October 28?
I'm doing the Yokohama Marathon, but for the

past three months I've been busy moving house and changing jobs, and I've hardly done any training. I'm not even sure I'll be able to finish the course within the time limit. You're someone I really want to meet and I feel that if you were standing at the finish line I'd be able push myself that bit more. The last finishing time is 3:00 p.m. I wonder if you could be at the finishing line at Pacifico Yokohama from about 2:30 to 3:30?

The client had previously trained almost every day, but hadn't been able to recently. He asked me to stand at the finish line to boost his motivation.

I had another appointment so said I could only be there from about 2:30 to 3:00. He said that was OK, so I accepted. This time constraint may have proved an extra motivation because it meant that to see me he'd have to finish within the official time limit. Anyway, he managed to reach the finishing line before 3:00 p.m. and so received his finisher's medal.

Despite being exhausted after the run, he immediately gave me my travel expenses. I was very impressed to think he'd been carrying the money the whole way. I don't mean he'd been clutching a handful of coins; the money was in a zip bag around his waist and because "coins would have jangled and been too heavy" he'd only brought notes, which meant I got more than my actual expenses. Afterwards he wrote me this thank-you message.

I hadn't done enough training and was lucky to finish within the time limit. What kept me going was wanting to see you and to hand over your travel expenses! Thank you so much! I was very keen to meet you after reading your tweets, and handing over your expenses was really important to me. Putting your money in my fanny pack was the first thing I did when I was preparing for the race. Thank you!

I wonder why the client chose me to be at the finishing line. Maybe he didn't feel he could ask anyone else. Or maybe he worried that if he did he might be too soft on himself. Knowing the person well might make it too easy to say, "Sorry! I couldn't do it! It was too much for me." That's just my conjecture.

That wasn't the last I saw of him. The next day I'd been asked to be host at the Mayoiga Event Bar in Hiratsuka, south of Yokohama, and unexpectedly, he came in. "I happened to be in the area," he said.

He was from Fukushima and said he was good at making steamed potatoes so the staff in the bar suggested having a steamed potato event with him as host for the day. The event went ahead—a steamed potato bar—and was a great success. Apparently, he got booked for another day too. You can never tell what's going to happen.

Incidentally, the nearest station to the bar had the same name as my former boss—the one who made demoralizing comments. I had to take a deep breath every time I saw the station name.

In the case of the marathon runner, I'd had to speculate about why he chose to ask me rather than someone he knew. In this next case, speculation wasn't necessary. The client stated her reasons quite clearly.

Request:
To have lunch with me and to go with me to file divorce papers.

To be someone to talk to on the way and while waiting (and to provide simple responses).

Reason for request:
I would feel lonely filing divorce papers on my own and would like someone to be with me.

Being accompanied by someone I don't know would give me unusual memories of the day.

I met her outside the restaurant where we were to have lunch. She told me it was the restaurant she'd come to with her husband on the day they registered their marriage. "But that wasn't why I'd wanted to come," she said. She'd chosen it for the food. I remember her taking her first mouthful. "Delicious!" she said. She sounded quite emotional.

After lunch we went to the council office and the client filed her documents while I watched from a seat nearby. When she'd finished she turned to me and said, "That's it. Everything in order."

She knew I was married and as she walked me back to the station she gave me some tips about filing divorce papers. For example, getting a divorce certificate makes it easier to change the title of a bank account back to your previous surname. That one wouldn't affect me, and although I don't suppose she was expecting me to use any of her tips, I enjoyed hearing about them. She also showed me her certificate. I'd never seen one before, so I found it very interesting.

I knew that one reason she'd got me to come along was that she wanted unusual memories of that day—but why was that important to her? Well, it seems that she didn't want to look back on the completion of her divorce as just a painful chore. She'd had to handle the whole depressing process herself—her husband lived a long way away and had done nothing more than send her documents, without even an accompanying note. It infuriated her.

She had another reason for asking me to be there. She thought it would help her to deal with things in an organized way. The idea of going to the council office was depressing and she felt that on her own she'd leave it till the last moment. She'd be in a panic, rushing through the door as the office was about to close. If she made an appointment to go with someone, then she'd feel more relaxed and be sure to get there in the early afternoon.

When we met outside the restaurant she introduced herself by her married name and asked that, once she'd filed her documents, I call her by her maiden name. So, when we said goodbye, that's what I did. It was an interesting day for me. I felt I'd accompanied her from one stage of life to the next.

My boyfriend has left me. Could you come with me to deliver his things to him? (I won't ask you to carry anything.)

This case seemed quite similar to that of the woman filing divorce papers. The client had broken up with her partner and didn't like having his things in her flat, but didn't want to throw them away. Although delivering them to him would be a hassle, she'd decided that was the best way and thought that arranging to go with someone else would help her get it over and done with. It seemed a good reason.

I met her at about 9:00 a.m. at the station nearest to where the man was now living. She was carrying a big bag. She said there was nothing in it that she felt sentimental about, just stuff that was too much bother to throw away. I liked her attitude: she seemed emotionally detached from the situation. She'd brought things like plates, which she wasn't sure how to classify—were they burnable rubbish, nonburnable rubbish or recyclable? She couldn't be bothered to find out. She didn't see why she should.

When we reached the man's new place, I waited a short distance away. It seemed to go surprisingly smoothly and she was back in no time. Perhaps she'd let him know in advance she'd be bringing his stuff that day. Afterward, we went to a café and had a snack. I listened for a while as she told me why they'd broken up and what a hopeless man he was, and then we parted.

Later in the day I got the following message.

Thank you!!
I went to his favorite café just now, sure enough, there he was. We had some tea together and chatted for a while as though nothing had happened.

I'd avoided the café since we broke up, but now (though I'm not sure anyone at the café realizes we've split up) I feel I can act normal. This is all thanks to you. I feel so much better!

I was very pleased that she was cheerful and that things seemed to be settling down between them. Even though I really had done nothing at all, I seemed to have been a kind of catalyst, and that felt good.

As a stranger being asked to do things that normally would be done by a relative, I get glimpses of human drama. I've dealt with a lot of cases; I don't remember many of them, but when a situation is sad or painful it tends to leave an impression, and these impressions seem to build up into something more general: a sense of what happens, or what can be done, in different types of situation.

I'm involved in a court case. I was wondering if you might be willing to sit in the court as a spectator, and then when it's over come and have a cup of tea with me. (It won't be depressing—I'll just want to relax for a while.)

The client was the defendant in a civil case at a court in Tokyo and wanted me to be there, but I suppose my main function was to be with her afterward when she was trying to relax. She thought she'd be stressed out after the day in court and would have plenty to say to someone who'd been watching the proceedings.

According to the client, the case was outrageous, and I felt sorry for her. She'd been suffering sexual harassment by her boss and, unable to put up with it any longer, had sent a companywide email about it, and now she was being sued for defamation. Her boss claimed that there had been no harassment at all, that what had happened between them had been with her consent, in fact, at her instigation. To me, listening in court, his claims didn't seem to stand up at all.

The client knew that she'd have to face her boss in court and that humiliating details would be made public. I suppose that was why she chose Rental Person as someone to have tea with afterward.

It also turned out that she'd been following my activities for some time and had often thought she'd like to make a request. She said she'd thought the court case would be a good opportunity.

She looked pretty miserable during the proceedings. Afterward, when she asked me if I'd ever attended a court case before and I said, "No," she said, "Great!" with a double thumbs-up.

She didn't mention the court case much when we

were having tea. I suppose she wanted to keep her mind off it and cheer herself up. She told me her husband enjoyed following my work too and said it would be nice if I dealt with a request from him one day. She asked me what interesting cases I'd dealt with and I told her various things I remembered. I think my being there probably helped her relax.

The following tweet about the case got quite a reaction.

🐦 @morimotoshoji
I was asked to attend court by a defendant in a defamation case (the suit had practically no justification). My role was not so much to make the client feel less nervous in her first court appearance, but more as someone to talk to afterward. I was with the client in the waiting room, sitting opposite a man, when I suddenly received the following message...

The message was from my client. I'd noticed her fiddling with her phone and automatically looked at mine. "The person in front of us is the plaintiff," her message said. I was excited. I'd never been to a court before. I enjoyed the drama of it.

Incidentally, as I said earlier, I always wear a cap. When I sat down in court the client's lawyer told me to take it off. I regretted having it on. I don't know if it was just good manners to take it off, or whether wearing a cap in the defendant's visitor seating might actually have reflected badly on the defendant.

Here's one of the responses I got to my tweet.

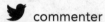 commenter
I found this the most surprising and thought-provoking of your cases so far. Even though the plaintiff's suit was very weak and the court's decision predictable, the process must have been very stressful for the defendant. Asking a family member to go with her would have been very awkward, though. It seems odd, but I think a stranger was the best choice—someone without any responsibility.

I won't add anything to that. I think it's a very convincing explanation of why the client wanted to be with a stranger rather than a family member.

In films and TV dramas, characters often set off on railway journeys while friends or family stand waving on the platform. One client wanted to have that kind of scene for herself.

Are you free on September 3? I've lived in Tokyo for ten years and now I'm going back to Osaka. I was wondering if you might come to see me off at the station, like a friend. This is a photo of what I mean. To create the right kind of atmosphere, I'd like you to come with me from my flat to the station and then come onto the platform.

Attached to the message was a picture of the kind of scene she had in mind.

She sent me this request thinking that she might get too emotional if a friend came. On the other hand, she couldn't exactly ask a complete stranger. Really, I was a stranger, but at least we'd exchanged some messages. I don't think she wanted to be seen off with any genuine feeling, she just wanted to experience this kind of situation. She was also a fan, I suppose—someone who followed my tweets enthusiastically—and she seemed to want to meet me before she left Tokyo.

I went with her from her empty flat to Tokyo Station and saw her off. I didn't have to pretend to be sad. As one of my followers, I think she understood me and it was nice talking to her, so it really did feel like a bit of a wrench to see her go. As I don't have friends this was an experience I wouldn't otherwise have had. And when I was in her apartment—a do-nothing person in an apartment with nothing in it—it all felt very unusual, entirely divorced from everyday life. Judging from the message she sent me later, she'd taken away good memories of her last day in Tokyo.

I felt lonely at the idea of leaving Tokyo on my own, but to be seen off by friends would have made me sad, so I contacted you. It was great—more fun than I'd even imagined. I felt like I was going away on a real journey!

I like to be free, so I normally do things on my own, but it was so nice to have the security of a companion. It was surreal having you in the apartment, and to be seen off by a stranger after ten years in Tokyo was great fun. Everything was wonderful. I'm so glad I asked you!

That wasn't the end of it. I heard through Twitter that the client (I'll call her A-san from now on to avoid confusion) had started a café in Osaka. I was going to Osaka so I thought I'd drop by, but I hadn't told her I was coming and when I got there the café was closed. I wondered if there was anything else I could do nearby—something to remember the place by—and suddenly remembered another request I'd received.

I'm living in Tasmania. A lot of bad things have happened to me recently and I'm really scared that next time I might die. It started with losing my phone, then someone used my credit card, and then a kangaroo jumped out in front of my car—the kangaroo was OK, but my car was dented and the windscreen was smashed. Next, a shovel fell out of a truck I was following so I swerved to avoid it and my car turned over—it was a complete write-off. There have been a lot of other small things, but to have two major accidents in a short period of time has really scared me.

This person worried that death was stalking him and had asked me to say a silent prayer for him when I was passing a shrine in Japan. There was a shrine near A-san's bar so I went there and said a prayer. I took a photo of the shrine and tweeted it. It seems A-san heard about this, indirectly, and then I, again indirectly, saw a tweet from her saying how pleased she was about it.

Then, when she was coming to Tokyo again, she contacted me with another request.

I don't know how to describe my relationship with A-san. We've met several times and have enjoyed talking, so we're not strangers, but, then again, we're not really friends.

This kind of vague relationship, which falls short of "friendship," can be quite convenient. You don't feel you have to worry too much about the other person—there's no sense of expecting anything from each other.

What if I did something to reduce the distance between us? I imagine that if the mental distance was reduced, the relationship would change.

I think it's normally reassuring in life to have particular names for relationships: friend, boyfriend/girlfriend/partner, couple, and so on. On the other hand, once a relationship is fixed, it seems to carry restrictions and responsibilities. If I'm somebody's "friend" and they consult me about something, then I feel I should give advice. Every named relationship entails particular things you have to do, certain expectations that you have to meet. If A-san and I were friends and there was no more contact between us, then there might be a sense of awkwardness. Since we're not friends, we don't have to worry.

★ ★ ★

As Rental Person, the way I interact with people is rather unusual, I suppose, but because of social media the number of people I "know" (without actually having met them) is growing at an overwhelming rate. Although they're not even acquaintances, without ever meeting, you share discussion topics. The idea of "followers" on Twitter and Instagram reflects a new type of relationship, with those involved often not even knowing each other's real names. The detached nature of the relationship also shows up in the practice of talking about followers in terms of numbers. It may seem odd from the point of view of traditional communities, but this type of relationship— neither friend nor acquaintance—can be very agreeable. It allows people to feel less isolated, while letting them avoid the obligations of more fixed relationships.

To give something a name is to distinguish it from other things. It draws a line. Perhaps Rental Person sits somewhere along the line between "friend" and "stranger." Where exactly Rental Person will be in any particular case depends on what the client wants. It's up to them. I don't do anything myself. I don't trespass on their territory.

4. not being tied down by money

Yesterday, I was treated to a beer and a betting slip at Oi Horse Racing Stadium. The slip cost 100 yen and my horse won. I was with the editor of the Keiba newspaper and I'd chosen the first horse he mentioned. My money had grown by a factor of 10 in 30 minutes. I immediately started thinking, "What if I'd bet 1,000 yen…or 10,000 yen?" That's the sort of thinking that leads to ruin. I'd better steer clear.

After I started Do-nothing Rental, I was often asked the following questions:

"How do you live? How do you make an income?"

"Why don't you charge a fee?"

★ ★ ★

Nobody can live without money. Unless they're very rich, they have to keep working to earn a living.

When Do-nothing Rental began, I had to think about charges. Obviously, that's the normal way for services to be financed, unless they can rely on advertising. So I thought about charging an hourly or daily fee like other rental services. But it was difficult to know what an appropriate rate would be. It was a pain worrying about it, and in the end I decided not to charge at all.

I thought Do-nothing Rental wouldn't be very interesting if the clients were my direct source of income. There'd be no scope for developing relationships, not just between me and the client, but with others as well.

At first, quite a lot of people sent in very original requests. It was as if they wanted to make it worthwhile for me to spend time with them. Instead of money, they were, in a way, paying me through their creativity. I wonder how different things would be if I'd decided to charge a fee. Many people these days are very conscious of getting a proper return for expenditure.

I'd like to think about the role of money in human relations, as well as other factors that are involved.

For Do-nothing Rental, important issues related to money are:

1. The critical issue of how to get income to continue (my problem).

2. The issue of how human relationships often require money (a general problem for everyone).

Although I did think about charging fees, I gave up the idea very quickly. I didn't even get as far as considering actual figures.

I didn't like the idea of an hourly rate. I hated the feeling that someone would be swapping money for my time.

I prefer being paid for getting something done, for achieving certain goals—payment by results.

It occurred to me that I should charge per request, but I had no market rate or standard to base my price on, and I dismissed the idea almost immediately. Different requests take different amounts of time, so on a per-request basis some clients might feel they hadn't got their money's worth. If it was a rate of 5,000 yen, for example, and we got through the request in thirty minutes, the client might think they'd been overcharged and try to get me to stay for three hours. I might feel the opposite, and want to get the request over as soon as I could in order to maximize my profit. This kind of scenario didn't appeal at all, with both sides being utilitarian, or simply stingy.

Money often simplifies matters—A gives X to B for Y. On the other hand, I felt that money might blur the real value of my service. So I decided that it would be best not to charge at all. If there was no charge, I could always maintain my do-nothing stance, and the client would never expect too much. Even if there was a charge of just 1,000 yen, they might start seeing themselves as the "customer."

I suppose the bottom line is that doing it for nothing seemed easier. It was a new venture and I was nervous about starting up and I wanted it to be as simple as possible. I'd be doing nothing, so it seemed natural to charge nothing. And if there was no charge, the client wouldn't be too demanding.

Those are some of my thoughts on money. This book was supposed to have a more detailed section on money, but this is the simple truth. I didn't really think about money that much when I was starting up. My main concern was to do something interesting. I had some savings, so I wanted to do something with them.

As I said in a reply to a follower's question:

I was wondering about your business model. How do you make a living? I'm sorry to ask. Please ignore my question if you like.

@morimotoshoji
At the moment, I'm living on savings. What I do isn't really a business. Maybe it's best to think of it as something I'm doing for fun (like a trip abroad I've saved up for).

I also wondered whether I should accept travel expenses. I soon realized that if I didn't charge expenses, and got a request to go to Europe or the States, my savings would vanish straightaway.

I didn't want my experiment coming to an abrupt end for a reason like that, so I decided to accept travel expenses.

I've thought about getting a sponsor. This is what Pro-Ogorareya did. I thought the sponsor could provide me with something (not necessarily money) and that in exchange I would, for a certain period, advertise their business on my Twitter profile. But I didn't handle it well. The person who wanted to be a sponsor offered me a range of options and I had to choose one of them.

I found this very stressful and was worried that things would carry on like that.

After that, I felt it might be easier to ask a sponsor simply to provide money. But then I thought, if there was more than one candidate, I wouldn't be able to choose between them. And anyway, it seemed inconsistent to be telling the world that I "do nothing," but at the same time trying to attract a sponsor, which was quite obviously "doing something."

On the other hand, if a wealthy donor was to appear suddenly and say they wanted to sponsor me, I think I'd accept immediately.

🐦 @morimotoshoji
Do-nothing Rental isn't "voluntary work." I'm not doing it out of the kindness of my heart. If someone offered me a lot of money I'd accept it without hesitation. I wonder if there's some rich person out there who'd provide a substantial sum with no strings attached.

I sent out this tweet some time ago because I didn't want anybody to misunderstand. The fact that Rental Person charges nothing doesn't mean it's a volunteer service.

It's not that I don't respect people who enjoy voluntary activities. It's just that I sense a lot of pressure if I'm called a "volunteer." If I said I was volunteering, I'd feel I was expected to be a person of pure goodwill. I'd feel a duty to ensure every tweet was touching and that every request was described with irreproachable fairness.

To avoid that kind of expectation, if I see a tweet that seems to suggest that Rental Person is a volunteer, I publicly deny it.

I really want to avoid being thought of as a good person. I'm absolutely not a good person and I don't want people to expect me to be. So if I feel I've been writing too many sentimental, heartwarming tweets (which really means I'm reporting on sentimental, heartwarming requests), I think *Hold on! I'm sounding too good*…and make a point of writing something that shows me in a more negative light. Here's one:

> 🐦 @morimotoshoji
> *Oh, so that's part of my role as a service provider, is it?* I think, when people ask me how much my train ticket cost, *Would it have been too much trouble to find out yourself before I came?* The prices are fixed after all.

On my profile I specify "expenses from Kokubunji Station," so why don't clients look the price up before we meet? In saying this kind of thing, I'm presenting myself as petty. I suppose I'm trying to control users' expectations. If people expected a really amazing person I might get requests well beyond my scope.

I wouldn't like to let clients down. I'd find it very stressful. I'd hate to read tweets saying, "Not what I expected," or "What a disappointment!" So it's best to keep people's expectations low. If clients come without much in the way of expectations, they won't be too disappointed.

Though I don't charge money, I do feel I get a kind of remuneration. For one thing, as I said before, there's the passive enjoyment and stimulation of hearing about people's situations. And when something interesting happens during a request, I think, *Great! I can write about that on Twitter.* I suppose this is my biggest reward. If I was paid money, I think it would be awkward to tweet about requests. Even if the client hadn't asked me not to tweet, I'd feel constrained. It wouldn't be right to make fun of people who'd paid me. As it is, I feel I can write what I want and don't hesitate to use a bit of dry humor. I didn't plan it that way, but that's how things have turned out.

I mentioned earlier that I get a lot of rather original requests, almost as if people are trying to keep me amused, and that this may be because they are not paying. For me this can certainly be seen as another type of remuneration.

One request I received was to be a nineteen-year-old girl for the day. I'd never imagined a request like that, but I enjoyed it. It was fun going around Shibuya, imagining I was a female university student visiting Tokyo for the day from my home, a long way away. The client seemed to enjoy tweeting about it. Here's what she wrote:

Yesterday I rented Rental Person. I asked him to be another me. I'm too busy to do everything I want to with just one me, so I created another. This other me went to Nishiya Coffee Shop and had the crème caramel I've always wanted. I'm so happy! (I'll go myself one day.)

This other me was very nice! She bought a book for me I'd always wanted and even brought me a present. I'd asked her to take photos through the day. Some were of a café she recommended. I'd never heard of it, but I'm looking forward to going there sometime. I'll go to LOFT lifestyle store too and have a great time like every girl student should.

In the early evening, I met up with myself in Ikebukuro and heard a bit about my alternate day. We both like to concentrate on eating so we didn't talk too much. I felt a bit of a generation gap, but it was fun. After we'd finished, my real me gave my alternate me—Rental Person—some flowers. This was something else I really wanted to do. The kasumisou I happened to pick up in the florist are symbolic of gratitude, apparently, so that was just right. Thank you very much, Rental Person, for everything!

This tweet mentions the Nishiya Coffee Shop, but actually its real name is Nishiya Coffee House.

The request to be seen off on a railway platform I talked about earlier was a similar role-play scenario. I've had quite a lot like this. It's like performing in a TV show.

With that type of request, I sometimes want to say, "Don't try too hard!" It's nice that clients use their imagination, of course, but when people put too much effort into trying to make something amusing, they often slip up. So I refuse requests where the planned effect is too obvious. This is often the case with "I've had this idea" type of requests from YouTubers. They usually don't work out and this makes things awkward for both sides.

As I've said, I refuse requests when my gut reaction is that I can't do it or I don't want to. It's the same principle when my instinct tells me that this kind of performance request isn't going to work.

For me, rather than invented scenarios, it's best to be used in real life, when people find themselves in unexpected situations and suddenly think Rental Person could be useful. A natural situation like that often seems to produce interesting requests.

Many followers seem to feel the same way and I get a real sense of support knowing that people want to send in interesting real-life requests. When I read a DM that says something like "Your activities are great. I'm a real fan!" I feel a little disappointed. If you're going to the trouble of sending a DM, why not send a request? By contrast, I get a wonderful feeling when a client is happy after they've made an interesting new type of request. They've been waiting for the opportunity and they're pleased it's gone well. They often tweet about it through their own account. That's my idea of a genuine supporter.

Of course, there are quite a lot of clients who ask me not to give details on Twitter about their requests or how things go when we meet. These clients have often shared with me their long-term troubles. I am grateful to them for that.

When people talk about Rental Person, the question of money always comes up. It makes me feel how interested people are in money and how it ties all of us down.

When I made my first request I was worried about not paying any money. I kept thinking, "Can I really take up so much of his time for the price of a cup of coffee?"

Sometimes I get requests from people who clearly don't have money. One of my first clients was like that. I'd gathered his situation from speaking to him. So when he tried to reimburse me for my travel expenses I said, "Don't worry!" I was upset at the idea of accepting money from someone who didn't have much to spare. But he insisted. "I want to do this properly," he said, so I accepted. Afterward, I noticed that he'd given me a one-way fare.

That client was a student, and of course, generally, students don't have much money. I still occasionally get requests where I don't want to accept travel expenses and it makes me feel uncomfortable. It's selfish, really. I just like to be able to accept travel expenses without worrying. So when there's something about a request message that makes me feel the sender doesn't have any money, I often refuse. For example, a question like "Are travel expenses one-way or return?" suggests the person is concerned about cost, which puts me off immediately (the answer is return, of course). This shows just how lacking in "volunteer" spirit I am.

My costliest travel bill so far has been a return trip to Fukuoka. I think it was about 50,000 yen by plane from Haneda. I didn't use a low-cost airline. The nature of the request is confidential; it was very important for the client, so I suppose they thought it was worth spending that amount of money.

I guess the farther people are from Kokubunji the more cautiously they weigh up the expense of my travel against the nature of their request. I sometimes sense people making this kind of calculation.

For example, I get some requests that seem partly, or purely, for the client's PR purposes. Once I'd become more well-known, bars began to ask me to act as host for the day, presumably thinking that I might attract customers. But I always think, *What if I have the opposite effect, and people stop coming?* So I make it clear when I accept such requests that I'm a very ordinary person and my being there won't mean anybody comes.

I wrote this tweet about travel expenses:

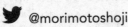 @morimotoshoji
As long as I'm paid travel expenses, I can go abroad. But acceptance of any request depends on the content. The most distant location of any request so far is Trinidad and Tobago. It was a request to accompany someone on a trip there, but I refused because of concerns about safety. The farthest I have actually traveled so far to handle a request is Fukuoka.

The Trinidad and Tobago request was from someone who said they'd asked all their friends to go, but none of them would. I expect they all said no for the same reason I did. I'm very sensitive to issues of security and I'm extremely delicate, so if anything unfortunate happened I'd probably keel over and die on the spot.

@morimotoshoji
The other day a client said, "I like being able to chatter on like this, or stay silent, just as I want.

RENTAL PERSON WHO DOES NOTHING

It takes years to build up a friendship that allows you to do that. And it costs money along the way. But with Rental Person I can behave like that right from the start. It's a real luxury!" I'd never realized before that Rental Person could have a cost-cutting effect.

It had occurred to me to look at this do-nothing service as an easy, low-cost way for someone to find a person who'd relate to them in the right way. But I'd never thought of a cost comparison with friendship. I'd always thought of Rental Person as something quite different to friendship. But here was someone equating Rental Person with a long-term friendship. It gave me a new perspective. I'd never thought that clients would see Rental Person as someone they could feel so relaxed with. Not that all of them do, of course.

The request had been to go shopping together, but I was late and by the time I got there the client had almost finished. So I went along to have a bit of cake at a café. I suppose the way I just did whatever the client wanted was rather like the behavior of a long-term friend.

I don't regard Do-nothing Rental clients in that way. I don't relax with them. That's not to say I feel uncomfortable with them. It's simply that, as requested, I do nothing, and think nothing.

The client said that to build a strong relationship with a friend took years and a lot of incidental expenditure. The good thing about Rental Person was being able to skip all that. They took the view that building and maintaining a relationship involves costs in terms of time, energy and money. From that perspective they seemed to think that Rental Person gave good cost performance. It struck me as a very fresh idea—a new way in which Rental Person adds value.

It would be misleading to say we pay for friendship, but friends certainly cost money. If I went out eating and drinking with someone and they always paid, then it wouldn't feel like friendship.

I don't really know how to define "friend" or "friendship," and I suppose different people would define them in different ways. But it seems to me that being with friends often involves getting out your wallet. You may go to a restaurant with friends, for example. And when you do, you share the bill, so that you have a balanced relationship. You don't want there to be debts on either side.

If you play a computer game at someone else's house, then it may not seem as if it's costing you anything, but if you live some distance away, then you have to pay for the train or bus to get there. And if you have snacks or drinks, then you probably share the cost.

But just going to someone's house once to play a game doesn't guarantee a real friendship. You'd have to keep meeting up and every time there'd be a cost involved. I know I'm sounding stingy; the point is simply that building and maintaining friendships involves spending time and money.

And besides financial cost, there are costs in terms of emotion and energy. Friends often lend things to each other. In Japan, this happens a lot with manga books. I did that with colleagues I got on with at the company I worked for. I'm not the type of person who wants to read something just because someone recommends it to me—I'd borrow it just because it seemed unfriendly not to. And if you borrow a book you have to read it, and when you give it back, you have to give comments. If you didn't enjoy it, you either have to lie and say you did, or you have to choose your words very carefully so as not to harm your relationship. I find all this kind of thing very stressful.

I suppose this psychological burden is the cost of adapting to the other person. As I said earlier on, I'm bad at building relationships within a fixed community, and I think one reason for this is that I can't easily adapt. I guess this makes the mental cost of relationships greater than it would otherwise be.

To reach the stage where you can just be yourself

with the other person takes a lot of time and energy. You probably argue sometimes, or spend long periods hesitating whether to say things or not. And this is all a type of psychological cost that mounts up over time until you reach the day when you can say without reservation, "That manga I borrowed, it was garbage."

So I think you could certainly say that skipping the whole process would cut costs, financial and emotional. That, at least, was how this particular client saw it. My not doing anything meant there was no pressure on her. It was interesting to find someone who thought like that.

Here's another client who felt similarly. A tweet about this got over 400 likes.

I'd like you to eat with me—something I've cooked myself.

Place: My room. I live with my parents and elder brother.

Time: Anytime on a weekend or public holiday.

Reason: Cooking for people satisfies my craving for approval. But if I just keep cooking for a friend, there'll come a time when they just take it for granted. So I'd like to cook for Rental Person. I'm not sure whether eating will fit with your definition of doing nothing, but please think about it!

When I'm asked to watch someone work or study, they often provide manga, to give me something to pass the time. I normally read them, but I never give opinions about them and nobody ever asks me to. If I want to, I play with my phone instead of reading. I haven't asked for the manga, after all. The client has simply provided them and has no particular expectation that I'll do anything. So I don't have to worry about it, which means there's no mental cost. It's very easy.

🐦 @morimotoshoji
Today I was taken to a ramen place by manga artist Kaoru Nagahori. I had some nice ramen, then went with her to her workroom where I read manga and answered occasional questions. I was also told to name her book in a tweet so that it would come up in tweet searches. Her workroom was full of popular manga books and I could read whatever I liked. It was strange and exciting to be able to use a manga artist's workroom as if it was a manga café. Most of the time she just worked away silently, but now and then she'd shout something like "It's great having someone here!" Then she'd

mutter things like "It's like being at a friend's house when you're small," "I wish everyone knew how nice it can be just to have someone there" and "It feels so good. Just right." I was pleased, though of course I hadn't done anything.

🐦 commenter

I wanted a person to watch me while I was working…so I rented one. A nice-looking young man came and sat behind me, reading quietly. Whenever I spoke to him, he answered politely. It was perfect. I kept muttering to myself about how nice it was. I really managed to get on with my work. And another advantage of having Rental Person come over was that I had to tidy the room. There'd been no space on the floor for ages— nowhere to put my feet. It was strange, though, to see someone from outside the family reading manga in my room.

Though I found lending and borrowing manga with my ex-colleagues stressful, I don't think I felt like that when I was a child. For Japanese children, manga are simply one of life's great pleasures. Any manga you haven't read is welcome, especially one your parents won't buy you. And it was just fun having friends.

There's certainly a difference between childhood and adulthood in terms of the cost or stress that friends or friendship involve. Friendship for an adult seems very complicated. Rather than all-round friends, people seem to have friends for specific purposes—friends to go drinking with, for example, or friends to play computer games with, and friends to go to concerts with.

I think this specialization of friendship is apparent in some of the requests I get. When someone asks me to go with them to a restaurant, a computer game tournament or a pop concert, I think that rather than having nobody at all they could ask, it's more a matter of not having a friend for that specific purpose. Unless a friend shares a particular interest, inviting them to come along might feel like asking a favor and thus puts you in their debt.

People want to enjoy life, and having friends for particular purposes allows them to do so. But this means friendship for adults often has ulterior motives. While working at my previous company, I realized that a lot of people took a very rational approach to friendship, but I never liked the idea of being part of that system. Not that any of my colleagues would have wanted to involve me in their lives outside the office.

* * *

At Japanese companies, one is expected to have a close bond with colleagues who are part of the same intake class at work, and going drinking together is almost compulsory. I found I couldn't really adapt to this. I couldn't be made to feel differently about people just because they happened to have been employed in the same year.

It was stressful to be expected to take the role of a friend in that kind of way. Now, though, doing nothing, I quite happily perform the roles assigned to me by clients. I don't at all dislike accompanying requests. They're easy. There is no lying involved.

If I wasn't Rental Person and someone asked me to go with them to a restaurant they felt they couldn't go to on their own, I'd be skeptical. *Why me?* I'd think and suspect some hidden motive. But when people use Do-nothing Rental, there's no suspicion. I feel secure. I know I'm simply being used as a tool to achieve a goal.

I wonder if you'd go with me for some ramen at the Ramen Jiro place in Ogikubo. I've never been to a Ramen Jiro before and I don't know how to order. I'd feel nervous on my own in such a busy place.

144

🐦 @morimotoshoji
A request to go with someone to a Ramen Jiro.
One of my very first clients asked me to line up
with them at a Ramen Jiro exactly six months ago,
so I've been to one before and could understand
how someone would feel nervous going for the
first time. My previous visit was on the first day
of Do-nothing Rental, so it was a six-month
anniversary. So for me it was a rather emotional
bowl of ramen.

Why is it difficult to ask a friend to go with you to a restaurant you feel awkward going to on your own? Maybe
it's as I said just now, if you don't have a friend for that
particular activity, you might put yourself in debt if you
ask someone else.

In Japan people are very conscious of reciprocity. Someone receiving a gift will try to reciprocate with a gift
of greater value. This mentality promotes a gift-giving
cycle, which helps to sustain relationships. I think people
look for similar reciprocity in terms of behavior between
friends. If A does something for B, then B will try to do
something more for A.

The writer Tomoaki Kageyama describes the sense
of obligation that a recipient feels as "a healthy feeling

of debt." For me, though, there's nothing healthy about it at all. The feeling that I have received more than I should from somebody is a source of extreme stress. If a friend does something for me, I have no idea how to repay them, let alone give them something of greater value. After all, I'm somebody who can't actually do anything, so I end up just carrying a burden of guilt. And with actions, as opposed to gifts, what makes matters even more complicated is that you cannot easily put an objective value on them. The two sides may have quite different ideas about their value; sometimes one side may not perceive any value at all.

I think people are tired of the cycle of excess reciprocation. They want to get away from the etiquette of insincere customs, such as summer and New Year gifts, and New Year cards. Although I don't want to criticize people who like these traditions, it's obvious that many others, for their own reasons, find them a struggle. I think this is one reason why there's demand for Rental Person, where there's no debt on either side, just payment for transport and food.

Social media has made the range of people's potential relationships much wider. Human relations used to be one-to-one and any personal exchange could be handled privately. But with social media, this can all quickly become common knowledge.

I'm going off on a tangent here, but it seems that the reason dating apps are so popular is that you can easily link up with people you don't know. It makes life simpler than trying to date someone within your community, where everyone will hear about it straightaway.

Rental Person also has the advantage of being someone you don't know, someone unconnected with your community. Do-nothing Rental is a way of achieving something without incurring any kind of debt.

Good evening! Please excuse this sudden message. I am giving 10,000 yen to people I like. Would you accept a payment?

 @morimotoshoji
A request to accept 10,000 yen. This person wants to give a hundred people 10,000 yen over two years. When people worry about my money situation, I normally put on a brave front and say something like "Well, I expect some will turn up somehow," and here it is, completely out of the blue! I was amazed!

I mentioned a similar case earlier, and, as I said then, people often send me Amazon gift cards and so on to say thank you. But this was real money, and not even as a thank-you! I gave the person my bank details and they transferred the money. I was delighted. It's nice to get gift cards too, of course, but an Amazon gift card can only be used on Amazon…so I suppose I think, *Well, why not give cash?*

Another thing I tend to be given, apart from Amazon cards, is 500-yen Starbucks vouchers. I suppose people feel they've given me 500 yen, but to be frank, I don't often go to Starbucks. Though I know it's kind of them to give me the vouchers, these days I'm constantly plagued by a feeling that I should go to Starbucks, even if I don't want to.

Of course, I know people think it's rude to give money as a thank-you. They feel it lacks refinement and they worry it might seem condescending. With its Starbucks brand packaging, a 500-yen voucher seems more sophisticated and so more suitable as a present. But the recipient would far prefer a 500-yen coin.

People also give me 100-yen coffee vouchers for use at convenience stores like Lawson or 7-Eleven. I don't buy coffees at convenience stores, so I never use them. I've begun to find it a bit stressful to thank people who give them to me. So, just to be clear, if anyone wants to thank me in that kind of way, I'd prefer money, even if it's just a small amount.

It might seem inconsistent for someone offering a free

service to say he likes getting money from clients, but when I'm traveling to meet people, there's often a choice between a quicker, pricier route and a slower, cheaper route. If I get 100 or 200 yen I can choose the quicker route without feeling any stress.

I've always wanted to spend a day on the Yamanote rail line circling central Tokyo. It would be quite cool to do it alone, but I think it would be fun to have someone to talk to. I wonder if you would come with me.

@morimotoshoji
A request to accompany someone all day on the Yamanote line. By the time we got off the last train, we'd done thirteen circuits. It was fun—like watching an ensemble cast in a reality show. But I felt awkward taking up space when the train was packed.

This was the most time I've spent on a request so far. I don't mind a request taking a long time. I don't see what's wrong with tying someone down time-wise; if both sides agree, it doesn't matter at all if there's no money involved.

★ ★ ★

Some clients like to give a financial thank-you. One gave me 15,000 yen for the time I spent with her at Tokyo Disneyland. She said she loved spending money on people and didn't normally have much opportunity. She'd come down from Tohoku for a friend's wedding at Disneyland and had planned to spend the day before the wedding seeing the attractions. The friend she'd intended to go with had had to cancel suddenly, so there was a spare ticket. Rather than go on her own, she asked me.

Besides paying for my ticket, the client also bought me a lot of nice food and gave me more gifts from Tohoku than I could carry. Then, on top of all that, came the envelope with 15,000 yen inside. The sum included travel expenses, but the return fare from Kokubunji to Disneyland was less than a tenth of that. Do-nothing Rental had only been going for a short while when I had this request and at the time I was just extremely grateful. These days I find it very interesting to see how different people feel about taking up others' time and how perceptions vary as to what is appropriate as a token of gratitude.

Of course, as I said before, I don't mind how much time I spend on a request. I never feel negatively toward someone because I'm with them too long. And Do-nothing Rental has always been free, so I never ask for any remuneration.

It's nice, though, when, after I've handled a request, the client tweets about it. It spreads the word, which is a reward in itself. And I always hope that people who tweet enthusiastically might buy this book. If they do, I'll get paid through the royalties that will appear in my bank account a few months later. What could be better?

The Disneyland client sent another request in December. She wanted to spend some money on a present for someone. She liked choosing presents, but felt that giving one to a friend or acquaintance might make them feel she wanted something back, so she wanted to give one to me. When I gave her my address, she said she was thinking of sending me some meat and rice. My wife and I are both lazy and normally use no-wash rice, so rather cheekily I asked if she'd mind sending that type. She agreed straightaway. "Certainly," she said, "I'll find the best I can. I'll enjoy looking." A few days later, a parcel of delicious meat and no-wash rice arrived from Tohoku.

Another request message said, "I want to buy someone a meal."

To be perfectly honest, this isn't a feeling I've ever experienced myself. But the client—again, a woman—said that her meals were always being paid for by men, which made her worry about how she behaved and what she chose. "If I pay, I'll be able to relax and eat what I want," she said. So I went along with her to a high-class restaurant in Shinjuku and ate my fill of very expensive food. I'd never seen a chef sautéing foie gras before, and I'll probably never see it again. It felt very strange to be eating that sort of food for nothing.

I didn't feel awkward about being given a meal like that. If it had been a friend I would have probably said, "Let's share the bill." As it was, I just accepted it. She wanted to spend the money on me, so I let her. It's the same when people give me money or gift cards. They want to give me something, so I let them. That's the way I look at it these days.

When I said this to the person who's writing this book for me, they said I must feel like an offertory box at a shrine. Well, I'm not sure how an offertory box feels, but I think that the situation with Rental Person is a bit different. People who throw coins into offertory boxes are wanting some kind of blessing or protection in the future. But for people who give me gift cards and money, there's no objective beyond the act of giving—they just want to throw the coins. Giving makes people feel good; it lets them feel positive about themselves. I can't think of a very good analogy; I suppose giving me gifts is quite like giving food to a pet. The pet just accepts the food.

★ ★ ★

Through this do-nothing service, I've encountered a lot of different perspectives on money. Everybody wants money and it's difficult not to feel stressed when you don't have it. So when we do something, we tend to think about financial benefit. I think that is why new ideas so rarely take shape. If I were to make money a top priority, whatever I did would be dull. Rather than avoiding stress, I'd become even more stressed. So I put the issue of money aside. For now, this allows me to do interesting things. And perhaps these will lead to something that makes money in the future. As I said before, if I charged clients it would lead nowhere. I think ignoring money has allowed me to have different values, which stimulate new and different ways of relating to people.

Rental Person has been described as "a new-age gigolo" and "a new-age beggar." I think being a gigolo or beggar are potential ways of relating to people, and the word "new" sounds good, so I feel quite positive about these comments.

🐦 @morimotoshoji
If I meet someone or the type of person who thinks any human activity must be a way of making

a living, I tell them I'm a writer. "I'm researching at the moment," I say. "Do-nothing Rental means I can experience lots of different things without much expense. It works rather well."

When I started this service, a number of followers asked me about my private life and in reply, I always tweeted that I had a wife and family, that my wife supported my activities, and that we lived off my savings. My only intention in posting these tweets was to answer their questions, but because I'd said that, people became less wary of me.

If I hadn't had my wife's agreement, I expect people would have looked down on me. Well, I suppose some are contemptuous anyway, but the fact that I have her support certainly seems to make people feel more at ease, and they probably don't feel guilty when they make a request. There's certainly no reason to. Financially we're OK at the moment, so no one should worry that a request is too trivial or that it would tie up my time.

Even so, some do worry. The Disneyland client was one of those. Besides giving me 15,000 yen to thank me for my time, she also encouraged me to go home early. Although she knew that I was married when she'd made her request, she didn't know that we had a baby. When I mentioned it at Disneyland, she told me I should go home. I was supposed to be with her until the evening, but in the end we said goodbye in the middle of the afternoon.

It had never occurred to me that someone might show concern about my family. It didn't seem necessary. Rental Person is my job. There is no reason for a client to worry.

Just to be clear, the visit to Disneyland was very enjoyable and the meat and no-wash rice the client sent us later on was delicious. If I get similar requests in the future I am sure I'd be very pleased to accept them. And I think it's marvelous that someone can be so kind as to say I should leave early because I've got a small child. All I mean is that, with Rental Person, that type of consideration isn't necessary.

When I worked at the company, I sometimes said to myself, *This isn't what I want but I have to do it for the money.* I couldn't keep that up. Later I tried dealing in virtual currency. I soon grew tired of it and gave up, but the experience taught me that money isn't just payment for work—it can come in lots of different ways. And then I started Do-nothing Rental, letting go of the idea of money altogether. Of course, some things are impossible without money, but having given up trying to get it, I've obtained other things, and I've realized that money is nothing more than a convenient tool.

I should add that it's entirely possible that my wife will stop supporting this do-nothing service in the future. My savings will not last forever.

Hello,
You were with me when I telephoned a lender I've been having trouble repaying. I've managed to make this month's payment in full! It's ages since I made a payment on time. I'm really happy—I feel almost respectable. I don't know if it's the excitement, but I feel a terrible urge to be wasteful. So please let me! It's up to you whether you use it or not.

 @morimotoshoji
A client who was behind with debt repayments has managed this month's payment. She's sent me another Amazon gift card. Seems to be a committed waste addict.

5. not resisting AI

I want to remember what I've got to do this week,
but normal reminders and memos never work for me.
Can I send memos to you by DM? If I send them
to someone I think I'll remember.

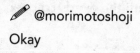 @morimotoshoji
Okay

Pay Nitori
Pay HIS

Done
Thank you very much.

People tend to be driven by a feeling that they must "do something." And once they've done it, they feel they must do more—better and faster. But when I started connecting with people as Rental Person, I realized that a surprising number were after something rather different.

I sometimes get requests to simply reply to a message using the exact words that a client has provided.

@morimotoshoji
I was sent a photo of a pet and asked to reply with the message "That is unbelievably cute!" I accept this kind of request if the words are given to me. Before I replied, the client sent a video too and also a picture of themselves, but all I had to do was simply reply with the words I'd been given, so that's what I did.

@morimotoshoji
I was asked to send a message saying "Wow! Amazing!" about something unusual that had happened to a client. They'd gone to a shrine at

160

New Year and chosen two fortune slips (omikuji) which said exactly the same thing. It did seem very unusual and I responded as requested. There can't be much doubt about what the client's year has in store. It was as though the second slip was saying "Look, I've told you once already!"

I often receive requests to send particular messages at particular times. At one stage I had huge numbers. It's something that smartphones have been able to do for ages, so why ask a person?

Humans don't do things perfectly. They're not like computers, which are 100 percent reliable, so with Rental Person, success is not assured. First, I have to accept the request. The client may worry that their request might be rejected, or that I don't see the message at all. Then I might not type the response correctly. These hurdles make the process more engaging for people. And because we can fail, success makes us happy, and that happiness can rub off on other people. Even when we make a mess of things, our efforts may help to establish a bond of trust. So in this context a human's low specs are a strength.

The word "specs" is normally used when talking about the functions or capacity of industrial products. Applied to humans, I suppose one would expect it to refer to attributes like running speed, competence in a foreign language, communication ability, or skills in a specialist area like the law or accounting. On that basis, I'm confident that Rental Person has very low specs—zero specs. I couldn't do anything, so I started "doing nothing."

When this do-nothing service had been going for about three months I got a request that generated far more response on Twitter than any I'd had before:

Please could you send me a DM at 6:00 a.m. tomorrow saying "gym clothes"?

Someone was trying to use Do-nothing Rental as a simple reminder service, but I replied "OK" and at exactly 6:00 a.m. I sent a message simply saying "gym clothes."

I took a screenshot of the correspondence and tweeted that it was the simplest request I'd ever had. It got an amazing response—over 20,000 retweets and 83,000 likes. Rental Person's follower numbers shot up.

At the time, I was just extremely surprised. Looking back, I think it was the human side that prompted the response. People liked the idea of someone sending a DM at exactly 6:00 a.m. It meant waking up five or ten minutes before the agreed time, getting the phone ready, typing "gym clothes," watching the seconds tick by and pressing "send" at exactly the right moment. People liked imagining someone going through this process, making sure it went to plan.

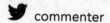 commenter
That's a pretty tough request first thing in the morning! Tell them this is useful! remine.akira108. com [an online personal reminder bot called Remine-kun].

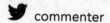 commenter
Eh! If that's a free service, it's better than a telephone wake-up call!

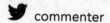 commenter
The idea of Rental Person sending a message at 6:00 a.m. brought a tear to my eye.

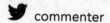 commenter
They could have used an alarm... But how kind you are!

 commenter
A volunteer doing something like that at 6 in the morning? Amazing!

Having done it, I know that it's not that easy to send a DM at an exact time. And, as I said earlier, Do-nothing Rental is not voluntary work.

There was a follow-up to this request. Here's my tweet about it:

@morimotoshoji
The client remembered to take the gym clothes, but then seems to have left them on the bus. I don't know if that was the reason, but they asked me to send a second message at 3:00 p.m., saying "Office."

After the popularity of the gym clothes request, I got a lot of requests for reminders like that—about thirty a day. I couldn't really cope with all that, so I refused most of them and I accepted the occasional one when I felt like it. For example, there was this important-sounding matter:

Excuse me. I may have sex today so could you send me a message at 12 to tell me to cut my nails?

Does sending messages come within the scope of doing nothing? I'm not very sure. When I got the gym-wear request, I thought it would be OK to see it as a type of "simple response." Some people may not agree, but as I've said before, it's difficult to draw a clear line between doing something and doing nothing.

Here's the Rental Person thread that's attracted the biggest response so far. I think it was popular because it highlighted something only a human could do:

Request: To bump into my dog on a walk and make a fuss over him.

Reason: My dog loves people. He goes up to people without dogs and wags his tail, but most of them ignore him, so he gets disappointed. People with dogs often make a fuss over him, but they're busy walking their own dogs and don't have much time, so I try to walk him away, but then my dog gives a little whine and sometimes tries to follow the other person. I don't want him to be thought too irritating so I cajole him into leaving them be, but he always looks upset. He is very positive and gets over it quickly, but it hurts me a bit every time his boundless love comes to nothing, so I always think how nice it would be if a complete stranger would give him some attention.

So I was wondering if you could make a fuss over him, pretending (?) to be a complete stranger who happens to be walking in the opposite direction.

🐦 @morimotoshoji
A request for me to have a chance meeting with a dog. Why? Because the dog is overflowing with love. He was really cute. The client said that the dog was sad after I left them at the station, his tail tucked between his legs.

This thread had 170,000 likes last time I checked. People must have been attracted by the cute photo of the dog and the nice request message too. It also happened to be Cats' Day in Japan (February 22), so dog lovers may have been feeling susceptible. Anyway, for me it was a request that put a spotlight not so much on dogs, but on the way humans love them. With the reminder request, people were surprised that a human had handled something that AI could do; I wondered what the reaction would have been if the dog request had been handled by AI. After I'd been petting the dog for a while, the client gave me a hand wipe. She said she always took some with her on a walk for anybody who touched the dog.

It was a very human request, kind in every way.

When AI first started to appear, a lot of people worried that it would destroy jobs. AI would be more efficient and so human workers would become unnecessary. People were also concerned at the prospect of care robots dealing with the old and disabled. When it comes to looking after people, perhaps it's only reasonable to want human care, irrespective of efficiency.

Somebody said that the demand for Do-nothing Rental as a reminder service is similar to the demand for humans in care provision. Personally, I wouldn't compare it to something important like that. For me, handling reminder requests is more like a kind of performance. It's about enjoying the absurdity of swimming against the tide of efficiency.

I don't think the popularity of the reminder tweet reflects a resistance to the spread of AI, it just highlights the fact that people find automation dull. They share a kind of AI fatigue. So when the gym-wear tweet arrived, it resonated with people—it was just the sort of thing they were waiting for. And I think there's a neat paradox in one human who can't rely on their own memory seeking support from another, who may not be able to rely on theirs.

I don't know why, but people seem to be very happy when I carry out this type of request for them. In about 50 percent of cases they send me an Amazon card or Starbucks voucher.

> 🐦 @morimotoshoji
> A request to write おつ [otsu—"Good job!"] when a client completed their 20,000-character graduation essay. They'd found it hard and six days before the deadline they hadn't written anything. But now they have reported completion. As requested I wrote おつ. The requester sent me a 2,000-yen Amazon voucher. That's a good pay rate—1,000 yen per character.

The client must have known that I didn't really feel what I said. After all, I just typed mechanically what I'd been told to and sent it off without thinking. But obviously, the Do-nothing Rental name has acquired a certain value. The client was pleased that someone reasonably well-known and with a bit of influence had taken the trouble to write them a message. "I've got a reply from Rental Person!" Being able to say that seems to make people happy sometimes. If it didn't, they wouldn't send Amazon cards, however much they appreciated the manual input.

Here's a slightly different type of DM-only request. It's stuck in my mind.

> 🐦 @morimotoshoji
> The client has been invited to a wedding, but isn't that close to the couple and doesn't want to go. The client doesn't want to say so directly, but, at the same time, they don't want to lie. So they'd like to be able to say they have a prior engagement with someone (i.e. Rental Person). Then, on the morning of the wedding, they want me to cancel the appointment. I'm ranking this top request so far on my scale of actually "doing nothing."

As the tweet says, the client didn't want to cause offense by refusing to go to the wedding without a reason, so wanted me to pretend we had an appointment on that day. I found it a very interesting request.

For the person who sent the wedding invitation, this use of Do-nothing Rental would make no difference at all. The client could still have written, "I am afraid I have a prior engagement," and the inviter would have been none the wiser. But the client wanted to alleviate their guilt by making out that there actually was an engagement. They wanted to be able to say to themselves *I made a real effort in refusing that invitation*. To me, it seemed rather like wrapping up a present carefully. Whatever the wrapping is like, the recipient is more interested in what's inside, but the giver feels satisfaction if they have made the effort to wrap the gift up neatly.

Personally, I think I'd have found it easier just to tell a straightforward lie, rather than go to the trouble of setting up a false appointment. After all, it was basically still a lie, even if the appointment charade seemed to water it down a bit. I suppose the client felt the process would put their mind at rest.

Or perhaps they simply wanted to remember their excuse. Forgetting lies can be very awkward. They often have to be kept up over time. I can imagine the client wanting to make the lie feel true by taking the step of actually making the appointment.

Sometimes I'm not keen on a request but feel hesitant

about turning it down because I've dealt with the client before. In that situation I sometimes hope that someone else will make a request for the same day and time. Even if it's not true, it's much less stressful to say, "I've got another appointment" than "I'm not interested." And, if I have given an excuse, I feel I can accept the next request from the same person without embarrassment.

The wedding invitation request gave me a lot to think about, but when the day came for me to send the last-minute cancellation I completely forgot, so in the end I really did do absolutely nothing.

Sometimes I get a last-minute cancellation from a client, leaving me doing nothing on my own. On one occasion this seems to have contributed to the client's success.

🐦 @morimotoshoji

A client canceled a request to go rowing in Inokashira Park at the last minute when they were suddenly called for an interview. They said the thought of having canceled an appointment to be there spurred them on to perform well. I'd find it hard to put their success down to the Rental Person effect, but clients are free to cancel at any time. So if people feel it may help...

Attached to my tweet was the following DM from the client:

I managed to get to the interview. Apologies again. The fact that I'd canceled made me think I must really try, and I did better than normal. Could be a useful strategy...

I once had the following request to act as an interpreter for AI.

This is a very simple request, but would it be possible for you to listen to some automatic vocal instructions on my mobile phone and repeat the numbers for me? There aren't many numbers, so I think it would take less than three minutes. I'm deaf so I sometimes can't hear on the phone, and I'm really stuck with these numbers. At the moment, I have no one with me who can hear, and so I thought I'd contact you. I wonder if you could possibly help me.

After meeting the client, I sent the following tweet with a screenshot of the original message:

🐦 @morimotoshoji

A request to repeat numbers given by an automatic voice—the type of thing you get when dealing with bank accounts. The client is hard of hearing and couldn't identify the numbers. As soon as we met, the client passed me the phone. I put it to my ear and said the numbers that I heard. That was it. It took about five minutes. A new Rental Person speed record.

This seemed the kind of thing a charity volunteer would do, and I felt it might make Rental Person look too good, so I hid behind the joke about the speed record. After that, the client sent a DM saying, "I felt rather embarrassed to have broken the Rental Person speed record, but I'm sure that there are others who face the same problem as I do, so thank you for sharing my request on Twitter."

As I've said several times already, although I don't have a charity volunteer outlook, through this do-nothing service, I have begun to appreciate the huge variety of problems that people face, and that sometimes zero-specs Rental Person can be of help.

With this listening request, if the client had just said, "I'd like you to listen to the automatic voice instructions and tell me what they are," I might have refused, on the basis that it sounded too much like "doing something." But the client wrote, "Would it be possible for you to listen to some automatic voice instructions and repeat the numbers for me?" When I read that, I got the impression that the client understood my do-nothing stance, and that encouraged me to accept it. When I feel that about a client, I tend to respond positively, even when the request may not quite fit with the idea of "doing nothing."

The Rental Person speed record was broken again within ten days.

I'm a university student. I can't get up in the mornings and at this rate I'm not going to get enough credits. I can't miss any more classes. Maybe I could get up if I was meeting someone. I wonder if I could meet you.

🐦 @morimotoshoji
A request to meet. We met. The client arrived at the meeting place and then went to their class. We parted the moment we met, so the Rental Person speed record has been broken again.

The basic function of Do-nothing Rental is to provide a person for a period of time. Typical requests that go no further than this include the "watching" type requests I've already discussed. For these I just have to be human in terms of size and shape. The specs are as simple as that.

> 🐦 @morimotoshoji
> I had a request just "to be" with someone who wanted to study at home on their day off, but couldn't concentrate alone. It took me 2.5 hours to reach the house and after that I just "was." I enjoyed being in the room. There were a lot of books, including expensive-looking hardcovers and some literary magazines. I put one of the books (*Momo*) back in the wrong place, which showed a lack of professionalism.

I often go to places where people live alone. They never say "I want to clean the house" in their requests, but asking me to their homes certainly seems to prompt a desire to tidy up. So, although I go just to "be" there, I have an automatic side effect of getting the house tidy. People seem to be embarrassed at even a complete stranger seeing their rooms in a mess.

> 🐦 @morimotoshoji
> A request to be with someone who has work to do at home, but gets lazy on their own. The client says it makes a real difference just having someone else there, even if they don't watch the work being done. Right from the start I've had quite a lot of this kind of request. It's becoming a standard scenario. A room-tidying side effect was apparent, as usual.

As Rental Person—a zero-specs human being—it normally gives me great satisfaction to make a contribution in such cases. But I do occasionally wonder whether the client takes me too much for granted.

> 🐦 @morimotoshoji
> I got a repeat request to watch the person studying. This time they didn't come to the station and so I made my way to the apartment by memory. I went straight in, did nothing particular while I was there, and when time was up, I left. I began to wonder whether this really made sense.

Sometimes when people ask me to come to their homes, they want me to eat food that they've prepared. One woman was interested in starting her own restaurant and wanted to know how it felt to have a stranger eat her food. My only impression was that it tasted good, so I said so, to which she responded "I'm glad."

She was married and her husband wasn't there, so the situation felt a bit unconventional. It was July 2018, soon after I'd started my do-nothing service, and I was feeling my way as to what "doing nothing" really meant. While I was there, the client's mother telephoned. The client was a rather unusual person and after talking for a short time, she said to her mother, "Rental Person's here. I'll put him on," and passed me her phone. There was nothing else for it, so I said, "Hello, Rental Person here."

"Are you having an affair with my daughter?" said the mother.

"No," I said. "I'm doing nothing."

It was rather an odd conversation.

Another type of situation that I'd classify as simply "providing a person for a period of time" is a business meeting. Here are tweets I sent out during a meeting.

🐦 @morimotoshoji
I've been asked to attend a meeting where people from a company I don't know are going to explain a service I don't know.

🐦 @morimotoshoji
Everyone's looking at computers and eating burgers.

🐦 @morimotoshoji
Some chocolate gâteau has arrived, just as the meeting was getting lively.

As you can see, I was doing absolutely nothing, but I've never felt so welcome at a meeting in my life. The company president had asked me to attend. He wanted to have a stranger there to break up the normal dynamics.

The people were told at the start that I was Rental Person. I think they tried to avoid jargon so as to make it all simpler for an outsider to understand. Perhaps I made it easy for them to picture potential users of their service. Things which are obvious to the service provider may not be at all obvious to the user. Perhaps my being there helped the participants to appreciate this and take a wider view.

Basically, all I did was eat hamburgers and chocolate

gâteau, but sometimes the president asked questions like "What do you think of this?" and "What do you think this illustration shows?"

"I don't know" was about all I said, not knowing anything about the company or its service. I suppose, by not knowing, I was in fact functioning as a kind of monitor.

When I started Do-nothing Rental, I thought it was most likely to be used in situations where, as in this meeting, I would be providing one person to add to a group of people. Rather than a meeting, though, I imagined myself in a party scene, or a barbecue, somewhere people were supposed to be enjoying themselves.

But once Do-nothing Rental got going, I found that by far the most common requests were one-on-one—almost all, in fact. I'd never imagined that. If it was me, I wouldn't ask to be one-on-one with Rental Person. I think clients are quite brave.

Though my relationships with clients are almost always one-on-one, use of Twitter means we're not alone—there's also an audience of unknown size. So I feel that Do-nothing Rental is made up of three elements: me, client and audience. Anyone watching can always go up on stage as a client, and a client can always sit in the audience.

I think people respond well to Rental Person because everybody can feel involved. Nobody thinks it's none of their business, so they really seem to engage with my tweets. They're very interested in the different ways that others think of using Do-nothing Rental.

Here's a tweet I wrote when I'd refused a request from an exam student who wanted a message of encouragement:

> 🐦 @morimotoshoji
>
> I used to work for an educational company and every day I would prepare math materials for students taking exams. Since quitting the company, whenever I see the word "exam" or hear people talking about exam preparation, I think, *What a load of crap!* I am sorry for the student who contacted me, but I'm afraid the whole idea of exams has become mixed up with bad memories of that experience.

One of Rental Person's followers who saw this tweet decided to send the student encouragement of their own. It was as though I'd rejected the student as she tried to get up on stage, but the audience had applauded her. I really am sorry for my reaction.

I mentioned before how I turned down three separate requests to accompany people to see the Emperor on his birthday. I suppose their decision to go together was like going with people they'd met in the audience.

Do clients ever feel disappointed when they go up on stage? Fortunately, not often—at least as far as I know. Perhaps I've managed to control people's expectations. Recently, though, followers have been saying positive things, and I think expectations might have gone up. If so, there may in fact be quite a lot of disappointed people.

I recently had a request to accompany someone on a walk through the streets and we spent five hours wandering around one area of Tokyo. The client didn't say much and, of course, I only made conventional responses. In fact, I wasn't feeling well, so I suppose my replies were briefer than normal. When we stopped, the client laughed and said, "We've been together for five hours—I'm sad we haven't talked more!" The client sounded as though they were joking; thinking about it now, I guess it's fair to say they were disappointed.

Do-nothing Rental clients normally say they enjoyed themselves. The stage can seem very lively. Expectations may be higher than I'd really like them to be, but it's difficult to know what to do to control them. If I just sent out boring tweets and there were no retweets, likes or replies, it would defeat the whole purpose.

I've thought about it quite a lot and have decided that Rental Person will continue to have zero specs. I won't try to get a conversation going with a client. I can't. And I'm sure "doing something" or "doing too much" could damage things.

> 🐦 @morimotoshoji
> When I was asked to act as a host at a "host club," I was advised not to refer much to the girls' (customers') appearance or jobs. I think hairdressers should get the same advice. I don't want to be asked whether I'm "on holiday today" or told "You look thin! Are you eating properly?"

I suppose these hairdressers want to seem interested in their clients. It seems excessive to me. Like many service providers, differentiating themselves makes them do too much. I've been to hairdressers who ask you to fill out a form about your hair worries, just like a medical questionnaire. All I want is a haircut. But when I say, "Same as last time," the hairdresser says, "Aren't you bored with that?" To me, this is a completely unnecessary intrusion.

Of course, it's their job, so a hairdresser is interested in hair, but, as a customer, I'm not interested in it at all. Haircuts are just irritating things that have to happen every month or two. That's all there is to it. If the hairdresser understood that, things would be much easier.

Recently, though, I've been going to QB House. Although it's cheap, they're professional and don't do anything odd. That's enough for me. I wear a cap all the time anyway.

When I think about Rental Person's zero specs, somewhere in my mind lurk the remarks my ex-boss would make:

"It makes no difference whether you're here or not."

"I can't tell if you're alive or dead."

"You're a permanent vacancy."

I suppose the basic specs for my job then were the ability to complete, in an efficient manner, any work that I was given, mainly editing teaching materials. Things were tense in the office at the time. Normally, producing educational materials is quite a routine process, with cosmetic annual adaptation of existing materials; but the syllabus was undergoing major changes and the company had decided on a fundamental revision of their materials. So what was required of the staff was not just editing know-how, but also the ability to develop effective new materials. There were regular editorial meetings and the focus suddenly shifted from individual work to teamwork. Ideas had to be developed with colleagues and presented to the boss. Project-planning and communication skills were required.

Some people thrive on this kind of teamwork, but I'm someone who just plods on in solitary silence. For anyone watching, it would have looked more than ever like I was doing nothing at all. The company wanted to outsource "simple tasks" and have staff concentrate on "high-level ideas" to be "creative." I'm afraid I couldn't come up with any useful ideas at all.

Once I had given up on creativity and started out as the entirely passive Rental Person, it was fun to find myself steeped in the ideas and creativity of people who send in requests.

So, what about my future?

There's not much I can say. Will I still be able to live my life doing nothing? I'm not sure.

I'm almost certain that as an individual I can live without doing anything. Many people are willing to give me meals as Rental Person, and I can find a place to stay just like that. I had a request in Osaka recently and when I tweeted about it, someone offered me accommodation straightaway. Ultimately, as long as people have food and accommodation, they can live. But I have a family and I couldn't leave them. (I might be asked to leave, of course, which would be a different matter.) I don't have to think about the costs of education yet, but my savings will run out eventually, so I'll have to establish a long-term means of supporting my family. Even though it's just a fantasy, really, the idea of "Do-nothing Family Rental" has some appeal. I am sure the demand would be lower than for Do-nothing Rental, but I can imagine requests for a family to stay in unoccupied houses while people were away. This wouldn't help with children's education, though.

In the first chapter, I mentioned Jinnosuke Kokoroya's notion of "payment for being" as something that triggered the idea for this do-nothing service. I think I was also, in a vague sort of way, influenced by the birth of our child. A baby has completely zero specs—it can't do anything by itself—but with the love and care of its parents and others, it lives. As I looked at our child, I kept thinking how wonderful that was. And I began to wish everyone could live like a baby does, behaving just as they wanted.

A thought like that should normally be discarded well

before adulthood. But there it was, and I feel it helped the Do-nothing Rental idea to take shape.

A baby is cute when it smiles, of course, and it's still cute when it's angry or bawling its head off. It's cute whether it's doing something or doing nothing. It's not trying to be cute, it's just acting naturally, doing what it wants. Wouldn't it be wonderful if the world worked like that, so that not just me, but everybody, could live just as they liked.

Maybe saying "not just me, but everybody" rings a bit false, as if I'm trying to make myself look good. After all, objectively, I think it's natural to want to take things easy when everybody else is working hard. I think it's honest to admit that. But actually, I'd prefer it if everyone else was living as they wanted, too. Then I'd just be following the crowd.

Perhaps I shouldn't be talking in such a philosophical way, but I mean what I say. A baby isn't just cute. It makes clear what it likes and what it doesn't. If you feed it things it doesn't like, it spits them out. It locks itself down. But as that perfectly cute, locked-down baby grows up, it's forced to accept our values—adults' values. Its lock loosens and its cuteness fades away. It's such a shame. It makes me wonder why it is that adults shouldn't just live as they like.

instead of an afterword

a conversation between rental person and his editor

Ed.

Thanks. About the redraft—could you get it to the designer this afternoon? Please say "yes" or "no" to the suggestions made in my email last night. The foreword and afterword can be sent later. Look forward to hearing from you.

RP

Basically YES. But instead of deleting the request about debt payment problems, I'd rather delete the afterword. I don't think I've managed to write anything worthwhile in the time given, so I'd prefer just to cut it completely. If that is awkward: YES.

17:14

RP

What is the point of a foreword and afterword? I don't feel the same as I did when the book was written…

17:26

Ed.

I think a foreword and afterword are like takeoff and landing. I think they add structure and make it easier for the reader to enter the writer's world. […] As a reader, I often enjoy afterwords, and I think it would be a shame to cut it completely. My suggestions are: 1. Not cut it completely—cut it selectively. OR 2. Redraft it by Monday, April 15. The final draft should be submitted by the 18th. It would be great if we could have a safe landing with one of these. What do you think?

17:35

RP

Thanks for your reply. I understand what you mean. But I think it's going to be really difficult. I know it's very late to say this, but I've begun to feel very strongly that for me to write an afterword is contradictory to my basic stance. Just letting you know how I feel.

18:45

Ed.

I understand. I'll contact you again tomorrow to decide whether to cut the afterword completely or maybe to put in one sentence saying, "I wrote an afterword, but doing so seemed inconsistent with my Rental Person stance, so I deleted it." It would be nice if we found some fun solution that fits with your thinking. Thank you for letting me know your thoughts.

19:24

Ed.

Just another thought: if we have no text, then perhaps a picture or something?

19:31

RP

Anything, as long as someone else does it.

20:58

★ ★ ★ ★ ★

about the author

Shoji Morimoto was born in 1983. He began his Rental Person service in 2018 and has since been hired more than 4,000 times. He's been profiled by many media outlets worldwide and has written several books, including *Rental Person Who Does Nothing*, which inspired a Japanese TV series. Morimoto lives in Japan with his wife and son.